THE LIGHT OF A THOUSAND SUNS

D1301834

It is not understood by those who understand it;
It is understood by those who do not understand it.

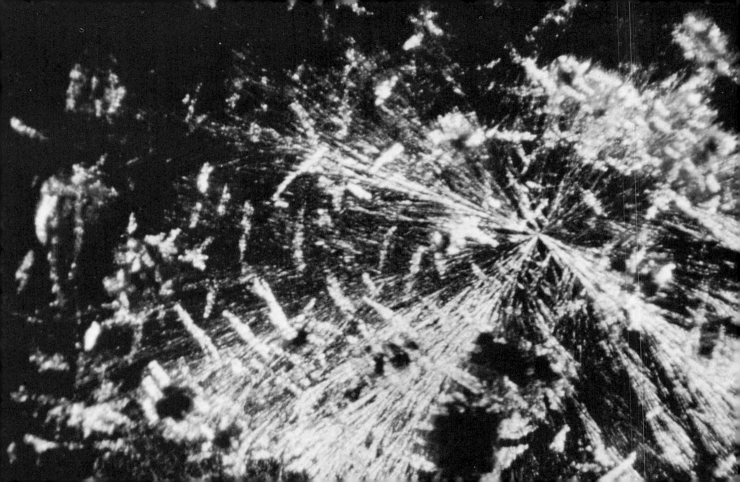

THE LIGHT OF A THOUSAND SUNS
Mystery, Awe, and Renewal in Religion

By Jacob Trapp   Photography by Bruce Roberts

Harper & Row, Publishers: New York, Evanston, San Francisco, London

FIRST EDITION

STANDARD BOOK NUMBER: 06-068431-3

LIBRARY OF CONGRESS CATALOG CARD NUMBER: 72-78061

Designed by Dorothy Schmiderer

Contents

To the Reader

Perhaps a good place to begin, if you read this book, is the last chapter, *"Sum Ergo Credo"*—I am, therefore I believe. To be is to believe.

Or you could start in the middle with Zarathustra, work forward to Christianity and then back to Judaism. Or better, begin at the beginning. Put your hands to the plough and don't look back.

> If the light of a thousand suns were
> to blaze forth all at once in the sky—

The remarkable Robert Oppenheimer of the Manhattan Project in Los Alamos cited this line and its context from the Bhagavad Gita when the first atomic blast was set off in the desert in southern New Mexico. Such was his feeling of the awesomeness of this blinding, explosive release of the power locked up in the atom. "He who can no longer stand rapt in awe is no longer alive," said Albert Einstein, who found in this experience the source of both science and religion.

Religions are absurd, or not completely rational or rationalizable. This point is not argued in the chapters to come, but illustrated. They are not for that reason untrue or quite without reason. They all, in one way or another, say Yes to life.

The still small voice of the intellect must be heard, but as an expression of the whole man.

The age of intuitive wisdom—roughly the millenium from Moses to Jesus, which includes such great figures as Isaiah, Zarathustra, Buddha, Lao Tzu, Confucius, and Socrates—speaks to us not from a dead past but from an unrealized future; and the age of science and technology, of growing materialism and collectivism, needs nothing quite so much as to listen to these voices.

We have been hacking away at the Wisdom Tree, branches and roots, and our children are a tumbleweed generation, sons of prodigal fathers, not knowing what they have lost.

In tameness is the wisdom of this world, in wildness its preservation. "Hath not God made foolish the wisdom of this world?"

"At the same time that we are earnest to explore and learn, we require that all things be mysterious and unexplorable, that land and sea be infinitely wild, unsurveyed and unfathomed by us because unfathomable."[1]

We may domesticate the gods, tame our world, and have an utterly sane and tame religion. But sooner or later wildness will again take over.

The later religions of kindness and love (how slow they were in arriving!) may not safely forget the earlier religions of fear and trembling.

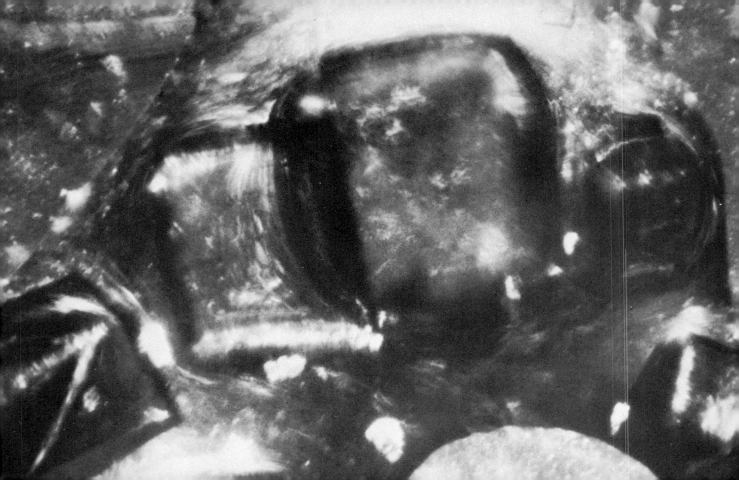

1. Where We Begin

Through the centuries the Jews have been heard to groan over the absurdity of their religion.

Absurd, and an intolerable burden to bear, that the God of this fathomless universe, in which the earth is a minor planet in one of myriads of solar systems, should have chosen a few nomadic tribes in Goshen as his people and promised them, in return for obedience and exclusive worship, universal dominion.

The towering absurdity of Christianity is that God became human and died on a cross. Tertullian in the third century, writing of the death of God on the cross, said: *Certum est quia impossibile est.* "It is certain because it is impossible." From this it was said that his idea of faith was, *Credo quia absurdum.* Absurd, incredible, impossible! Therefore I believe.

All religions are absurd in the sense of holding beliefs, making affirmations, despite overwhelming evidence to the contrary. They say Yes, when a No would be more rational, or easier.

What truth the religions have is not the certitude of reason or logic; but more like the sureness of the feel of an apple in one's hand.

The religions of men grew from a certain primary, speechless, and elemental awe. In the beginning there was much dread and terror mixed with that awe. But it was never just animal fear. Animal fears made no religions. It was the awe and dread and terror of a human being. It was the overwhelming tide which rolled over this little biped as he stood amid crashing thunder, or felt the earth quake, or looked into the fathomless depths of the starry firmament.

In this experience we are no different from our remote ancestors, as far back as they were human. We too can feel the tide flow over us as we stand before the *mysterium tremendum,* the stupendous otherness, the ineffable, the incomprehensible, the fathomless abyss.

Rudolph Otto, in *The Idea of the Holy,* calls this primary experience a sense of the numinous, a state after its own kind and irreducible to any other.

Dr. Otto lists and discusses in successive chapters such elements of the numinous as creature-feeling or dependency, shuddering awe before the *mysterium tremendum* and its majestic overpoweringness (often combined with an irresistible fascination), and the feeling of being grasped by something alive and compelling, like the consuming fire of love or divine wrath. Biblical literature has strong and frequent expressions of this sense of the numinous in the encounters of such men as Abraham, Jacob, Moses, Elijah, and Isaiah with the divine majesty.

A most striking expression of the numinous, both in its appalling frightfulness and its sublimity and grandeur, occurs in the eleventh chapter of the Bhagavad Gita, where Arjuna's prayer is granted to see Krishna in his divine majesty as an incarnation of Vishnu, instead of in his human semblance as Arjuna's companion and charioteer.

> If the light of a thousand suns were to
>   blaze forth all at once in the sky,
> That might resemble the splendor of that
>   exalted Being.

Arjuna, struck with amazement, his hair standing on end, bowed down his head to the Lord and with hands folded in salutation addressed him, seeing in Krishna's transfiguration the indescribable wonder and majesty of all the creatures of heaven and earth in this one divine form.

> I have seen what was never seen before
> And I rejoice, but my heart is shaken with fear.

He prays to be delivered and to see again Krishna's gracious human form.

Religions arise from profounder depths than the rational, are not amenable to reason, and answer to a need other than the need for logical demonstration.

Man is a creature who confronts the universe. In his aloneness he does this, and in awe and terror he is made as though nothing before it. He feels the need to be related, to yield himself to the whole, or through ritual to inure himself to the abyss and domesticate the gods. An altar is meant not only to make the worshiper feel himself in the mysterious Presence, but also to make it possible for him to bear it. At the altar one may draw near and still live.

So in that great passage about the numinous in the sixth chapter of Isaiah:

> I saw the Lord sitting upon a throne,
> high and lifted up, and his train filled the temple.
> Above it stood the seraphim:
> each one had six wings;
> with twain he covered his face,
> and with twain he covered his feet,
> and with twain he did fly.
> And one cried to the other, and said,
> "Holy, holy, holy, is the Lord of hosts:
> the whole earth is full of his glory."
> And the posts of the door moved at the voice of him that cried,
> and the house was filled with smoke.

Isaiah said,

> Woe is me! for I am undone,
> because I am a man of unclean lips.

Isaiah is overwhelmed, momentarily undone, but not annihilated. Rather, his lips are cleansed with a coal of fire, and he receives the commission for which he came.

The historic religions can only be discussed fully, descriptively, in terms of a rich complex of experiences. But basic to them all, humanly, is the sense of the numinous. Should that vanish, so would the religions.

2. The Rig-Veda: Poetry Believed In

In the later hymns of the Rig-Veda, if not in the earlier spells and incantations, we come closer to Santayana's idea of religion as poetry believed in.[1] The Rig-Veda, earliest complete collection of hymns and incantations for sacrificial rites, is regarded to this day by orthodox Hindus as a divine revelation breathed forth into the souls of poet-priests or *rishis*. Whether regarded as inspired revelation or a great human literature, these writings help one to comprehend some part of India's teeming and amazingly varied religious world.

To enter understandingly and sympathetically into the thoughts and feelings of men and women of long ago, although difficult, is perhaps no more impossible than to recapture one's own childhood wonderings and emotions, before the world of "it" overburdened and more and more obliterated the world of "thou." Although nothing can bring back the hour of "splendor in the grass" or "glory in the flower," we have "shadowy recollections" of a time when all things were personalized, when certain groves had their own awesome presence and aura of the mysterious, and when "the Lord went before in the sound of marching in the trees." When we read of great beings in the sky, clothed with stars, opening the sluices of the rain, hurling the thunderbolt, and driving the chariot of the sun, we are more likely to find a key in our own childhood as to how men once felt and viewed the world than in our later intellectual constructions and classifications.

From the northwest the Sanskrit-speaking Aryans swept down into India in successive waves of invasion and immigration, somewhere between 2000 and 1500 B.C. Some of the poems of the Rig-Veda were doubtless brought with them—spells, incantations, verses to be chanted around the sacrificial fire, transmitted orally by trained repeaters generations before they were committed to writing. Later others were added, until there were 1017 hymns, divided into ten books.

Much of this early, complete collection of sacred verse is like a dark screen of storm and cloud through which *devas*, shining ones, break forth like lightning or sunlight. *Div* may have been originally an exclamation, accompanied by a gesture of pointing —"There!"—wherever the fire or the radiance burst forth. So the name of the Hebrew Yahveh may derive from the exclamation *ya*, a simple excited "Oh!" evoked by some sound or sight of the Hidden One in passing, or of another world impinging on this.[2]

As hymns or poems for the sacrificial rites, the Vedas had to be chanted correctly by those who knew, sacred word after sacred word. The sacrificial offerings could be made only through the mediation of priests who controlled the shrine and knew the right ceremonial approach to the invisible being. There was an element of magic in this; that is, the right words, gestures, acts, performed at the right time and place, had power to compel, or to persuade, or to "conjure forth." Here we begin to hear the utterance of man's belief in his own powers and potentialities. That man could thus in some degree cope with the unseen powers all around him enhanced his confidence, his courage to be.

Ritual and ceremonial were thus a spur to the life-force. Also they intensified man's existence and added luster, interest, and excitement. Out of the loneliness of self, or the compactness and unrelenting scrutiny of the family group, a man could fling himself into the dance; he could realize in its anonymity an intensified individuality, in that now he was truly one among many and not merely a named member of a named group. Or he could lose himself in the rhythms of dance and chant, and feel himself at one with all the others and with the great mysterious world around him. The savage who made fire, it has been said, also made ritual his most important artifact.

To read and reread the hymns of the Rig-Veda is to come to the realization that the gods of a growing oral tradition, the gods of these great poems written by poet-priests of nature and the ineffable, are not intellectual constructions or somber items of a creed. They are dramatic story elements of actual encounters and subjective emotions, woven and rewoven by the human imagination into a changing and growing pattern by poets responding to the grandeur of the universe and the streaming inexhaustible wonder of existence.

> I am the necessary angel of earth,
> Since in my sight, you see the earth again,

wrote Wallace Stevens, in *The Auroras of Autumn,* of the poetic imagination. Imagination is also the necessary angel of the religions, without which they could not have come into existence or achieved significance and grandeur.

The gods and goddesses of the Rig-Veda, still so very much alive in India, were a symbolic structure of the imagination, growing out of actual encounters with the world and having power of suggestion precisely because they were not crassly or superficially literal.

It would be a gross oversimplification, then, to say that these horsemen and herdsmen who thundered down into the Indian peninsula were literal sun-worshipers, fire-worshipers, wind-worshipers, or worshipers of the various powers that manifested themselves in these. It would be an oversimplification, too, to say that they were worshipers of the one power or being who took these various forms and was given these names. An evolution took place, during the course of which all these various names or ideals coexisted in the minds of some worshipers. To read their songs is to become convinced that the authors (who sometimes compared their craft to that of the carpenter, the weaver, or the rower of a boat) were, in most instances, quite beyond the worship of phenomena or of separate and distinct personalized powers behind the phenomena.

In the Rig-Veda, for instance, there are many hymns addressed to the sun, by whose energy we live—as we learn from the very latest textbooks. This is nothing new; it was apprehended by men the world over millenniums ago. (In the House of Hades there is no sun.) The interesting thing about these poets of the Rig-Veda is that they freely adopt many names for that *deva* or shining one who is the sun, as though dimly apprehending at first, as they came to see clearly later on, that names are but names.

One name was Surya, the charioteer, guider of the steeds that took the sun on his daily journey. Another was Pushan, the shepherd's sun, a humbler kind of charioteer who drove goats instead of horses. Another was Mitra (cf. Mithra of the Persians), who rode with Varuna, the lawgiver, on the same golden chariot. Still another was Savitri, the enlivener, who makes man's daily life possible here on this earth. The most sacred verse of the Vedas, addressed to Savitri at dawn, is still recited in India and is said to be the oldest prayer in the world in continuous use: "Let us meditate upon the adorable splendor of Savitri. May he quicken our minds!"

There were various other names for this active, light-giving, warmth-giving, energizing being, the sun. The sun is addressed as the dispeller of darkness, the light-giver who awakens at dawn and is "the giver of daily life." He causes things to spring forth and grow, and is thus the nourisher, the giver of man's daily bread. He is addressed also as the Creator, as though light were the beginning and the instrument of creation. And then, in an attribute that seems to reach out beyond the sun, although the same names are used, he becomes the All-Seeing One, who scatters the stars from the sky and reads the secret thoughts of men.

> The constellations scatter like thieves,
>   together with their beams,
> Before the all-beholding Sun.[3]

And then, beyond this, he is thought of as transcending all the other gods, upon whom he bestows life and immortality.

Obviously, this is not simple sun worship, any more than the hymns to Ushas, the dawn goddess, indicate a naïve belief that the dawn is a woman, or—as in other hymns —that dawn and dusk are twin sisters.

> Dawn, like a bride, unveils her beauty.
> Heaven's lovely and obedient daughter,
> She comes by her known paths, never failing.
> Arrayed in garments of light,
> She steps over the eastern threshold.
> Smiling upon all,
> Kinfolk or stranger, humble or high,
> She mounts her car
> And goes forth to gather the day's riches.[4]

Here, as she mounts her car, Sister Dawn is transformed into Brother Sun. And the necessary angel opens men's eyes to the beauty of the world.

To make the symbolic structure complete, since there is also the violently destructive in nature, the Rig-Veda includes many hymns as well to the death-dealing
powers. Of them the term *asura* (endowed with breath) is used, instead of *deva*
with its connotations of the kindly and bright. Although the givers of life were also
givers of death, there were, as their emmissaries, these lesser beings who reveled in
the destructive work assigned to them. Such were the Maruts, the storm gods,
sometimes sung so magnificently—the "pounders" who came rushing headlong
wielding thunder and lightning, rending mountains, breaking trees, killing men and
cattle and destroying their dwellings. The "artifact of ritual" seems to be but the
skeleton of many of these hymns of the Rig-Veda, which are clothed and transfused
with the imagery of great poetry.

> I saw the celestial Herdsman, who never rests,
> Approaching and departing on his pathways.
> He, clothed in gathered and diffused splendor,
> Within the worlds continually travels.[5]

The varied and ascending range of attributes and powers ascribed to the sun is sung
in a similar way in other hymns to other beings. Indra, the storm god, Agni, fire, Varuna,
law and natural order, Dyaus (cf. Zeus) the sky, and so on in a great company, are all
in turn exalted to the heights and invoked as supreme. Each may fill the whole horizon
for the worshiper. In each of them men standing in awe, adoring beauty and benefi-
cence, were looking beyond the named and the conceptual to an ineffable supreme.

Or, in other less truly worshipful times, they were taking them for granted and using them as a shield against the abyss of the ultimate.

No one of these gods in India seemed able to hold the exclusive position of being the one arrow alone that pointed to the ultimate. In the later Atharva-Veda we find a verse addressed to Agni which reads—and surely there is a realization here that names are but names—

> In the evening Agni becomes Varuna;
> He becomes Mitra when rising at dawn;
> Having become Savitri, he ascends into the sky;
> Having become Indra, he warms the heavens at noon.[6]

In order to point to something more than one name suggests, pairings of names begin to take place. So Mitra and Varuna become Mitravaruna, light- and lawgiver.

In their intuitive and imaginative explorations of reality, the Hindu sages and poets could cling but briefly to one name, to one mythical personalized being. They could stand in awe before and celebrate the gods of the grandeur of mountains, rivers, and skies because they were symbols, names for manifestations of a Power and a Mystery within all and beyond. In one of the later hymns of the Rig-Veda we encounter this striking stanza:

> You will never know him who created these things;
> Something stands between.

Enveloped in mist and with faltering voice,
The poets walk along rejoicing in life.[7]

And in another, the famous creation poem of the Rig-Veda, the mind boldly traverses the nether world of the gods and stands poised before the Fathomless:

Then was not non-existent nor existent;
There was no realm of air, no sky beyond it.
What covered in, and where? and what gave shelter?
Was water there, unfathomed depth of water?

Death was not then, nor was there aught immortal;
No sign was there, the day's and night's divider.
That One Thing, breathless, breathed by its own nature:
Apart from It was nothing whatsoever.

Darkness there was; at first concealed in darkness
This All was undiscriminated chaos.
All that existed then was void and formless.
By the great power of Warmth was born that Unit.

Thereafter rose Desire in the beginning:
Desire, the primal seed and germ of Spirit.
Sages who searched with their heart's thought
Discovered the existent's kinship in the non-existent.

> Traversely was their severing line extended.
> What was above it then, and what below it?
> Begetters, mighty forces, free action here, and energy up yonder:
> Who knows and can declare it, whence came and was born this creation?
>
> He, the first origin of this creation,
> Whether he formed it all or did not form it,
> Whose eye controls this world from highest heaven,
> He verily knows it; or perhaps he knows it not.[8]

This is a hymn of the abyss of mystery, of the superpersonal One, of which the personal is but a mode or a manifestation. The gods too are but manifestations.

> There is no Indra, who has ever seen him?
> To whom are we to direct our song of praise?[9]

After every name eventually, came such a No. And yet, also, to all names a Yes, to all mythical beings a Yes, as part of the teeming and kaleidoscopic manifestations of the One Nameless Unknown, fathomless, not here nor there but everywhere.

To the beyond, the ineffable, the people of India drew close through their many gods, avatars, mahatmas. They saw the fathomless, timeless Inbreather and Outbreather of universes as beyond the Himalayas, beyond the depths of the stars, not only transcendent but also immanent, within all, the Dweller in the Innermost.

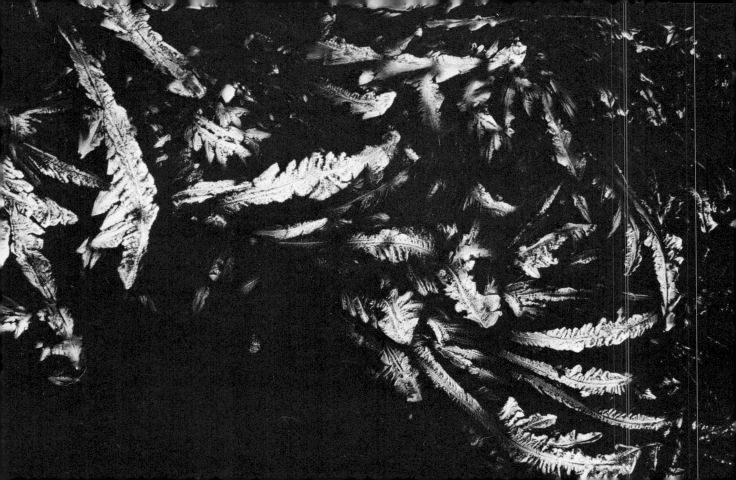

3. Krishna, Arjuna, and The Forest Sages of India

Perhaps nowhere is the absurdity of religions more immediately apparent than in the opening passages of one of the classics of religious literature, the Bhagavad Gita. "The pearl of great price in the ocean of Brahmanical teaching," it has been called; also, the Sermon on the Mount of India.

The Bhagavad Gita was inserted into the Mahabharata, an epic of gods, kings, and warriors, to give it a dramatic setting in a popular folk literature. The metal in which this jewel is set, one might say, is the iron of clashing spears. War is about to break out betwen two royal households and their subjects. The two armies are arrayed for fratricidal combat: on the one side the Pandavas, on the other their cousins the Kurus.

Arjuna, royal warrior, son of Pandu and the commander of the army of the Pandavas, is sickened by the thought of spilling the blood of his kinsmen.

There Arjuna saw standing fathers and grandfathers,
uncles, brothers, sons and grandsons,
also teachers and companions.
Overcome with compassion, he said sadly:
When I see my own people arrayed for fight, O Krishna,
my limbs quail, my mouth goes dry,
my body shakes and my hair stands on end. . . .
How can we be happy, O Madhava, if we kill our own people?
.   .   .   .   .

Alas, what a great sin have we resolved to commit
in striving to slay our own people through our greed for the pleasures of kingdom!
Far better would it be for me if the sons of Dhritarashtra,
with weapons in hand, should slay me in battle
while I remain unresisting and unarmed.

Having spoken thus on the battlefield,
Arjuna sank down on the seat of his chariot,
casting away his bow and arrow,
his spirit overwhelmed by sorrow.

But Krishna, his divine charioteer in human form, incarnation of Vishnu, dissuades him from this "unmanliness" and persuades him to do the duties of his castle.

Krishna uses the stock arguments, in part, of "your enemies will think you are a coward," "dishonor is worse than death," "nothing is higher for a Kshatriya [warrior] than a righteous war."

But Krishna's main argument, his "religious" persuasion, is that of the famous *tat tvam asi,* "that art thou" doctrine of the Upanishads.

> He who thinks that this one slays
> and he who thinks that this one is slain,
> both of them fail to perceive the truth;
> this one neither slays nor is slain.
>
> He is never born, nor does he die at any time,
> nor having once come to be does he again cease to exist.
> He is unborn, eternal, permanent, and primeval.
> He is not slain when the body is slain.[1]
>
> .   .   .   .   .
>
> Just as a person casts off worn-out garments
> and puts on others that are new,
> even so does the embodied soul
> cast off and take on flesh anew.
> Weapons do not cleave this self;
> fire does not burn him;
> waters do not make him wet;
> nor does the wind make him dry.[2]

The Bhagavad Gita, it is said, was the udder through which streamed the milk of the Upanishads. The unknown author of the Lord's Song, in having Krishna argue that the slayer does not slay, nor is the slain slain, was giving his version of the immanent-transcendent, the *tat tvam asi* doctrine of the Upanishads. He was quoting directly, in fact, from the Katha Upanishad:

> The knowing self is never born,
> nor does he die at any time.
> He sprang from nothing and nothing sprang from him.
> He is unborn, eternal, abiding and primeval.
> He is not slain when the body is slain.
>
> If the slayer thinks he slays,
> or if the slain think that he is slain,
> Both of them do not understand.
> He neither slays, nor is he slain.[3]

Arjuna, therefore, confident of virtue, may take up arms and perform the duties of his warrior caste on the battlefield. His sword cannot reach the soul, the real and deathless self of his opponent. (This Mahabharata setting of clashing spears was interpreted allegorically by Mahatma Gandhi: the struggle is between good and evil; the battlefield is the human heart.)

There is the mortal empirical self, a flux of states belonging to the world of *maya*, or illusion. There is the essential immortal self, "the knowing self who is never born and never dies."

> Sitting, he moves far;
> Lying, he goes everywhere.
>
> Unmoving, one, it is swifter than the mind.
> Although standing still, it outstrips those who run.
> It moves and it moves not;
> It is far and it is near;
> It is within all this and it is outside all this.[4]

This is the immanence, within the transient individual, of the eternal, the transcendent. *Tat tvam asi.*

> That which is the finest essence,
> The whole world has that for itself.
> That is Reality,
> That is Atman.
> That art thou.[5]

The individual essential self is identical with the infinite Brahman. A passage often cited about this, from the Chandogya Upanishad, reads:

He who consists of mind, whose body is life, whose form is light, whose conception is truth, whose self is space, containing all works, all desires, odors and tastes, encompassing all, the unspeaking, the unconcerned—this Self of mine within the heart is smaller than a grain of rice, or a barley-corn, or a mustard-seed, or a grain of millet, or the kernel of a grain of millet; this Self of mine within the heart is greater than the earth, greater than the atmosphere, greater than the sky, greater than all these worlds.[6]

The infinite transcendent Brahman is utterly beyond our conception or understanding. "Not by speech, not by mind, not by sight can He be apprehended. How can he be apprehended otherwise than by one's saying, 'He is'?"[7] Yet this is essentially what we are. "This shining, immortal person who is in the body, he, indeed, is just this self. This is immortal, this is Brahman, this is all."[8]

The idea of an indestructible monad in the individual—referred to in several of the Upanishads as "a person the size of a thumb" who "resides in the middle of the body," but in the passage cited above as "smaller than the kernel of a millet seed"—is a kind of ultimate refinement of animism. Although an absurd doctrine where it asserts the unreality of slaying or being slain, it has been to unnumbered millions of Hindus the answer to profoundest need, a self-affirmation and life-affirmation over against the transient flux, the conditional, the world of maya.

The first significant meeting of East and West took place when the self-confident Aryan herdsmen swept down into India and encountered the darker-skinned Dravidians, only to be conquered by the land and people they had invaded. The massive impact in India of uncontrollable nature overwhelmed the idea that man could be the independent master of his surroundings and the measure of all things. The earlier exuberance and self-confident assumptions of the invaders were shaken by India's majestic Himalayas, her fiercely blazing suns, her rainy seasons and floods, her teeming jungles with their rampant creepers and dark masses of trees.

> Tyger, tyger, burning bright
> In the forests of the night,
> What immortal hand or eye
> Could frame thy fearful symmetry?

The invaders were profoundly affected also by contact with an older Dravidian culture, the origins of which are lost in cities silted over by the winds and the rivers. Here they encountered the idea of transmigration of souls, of life-monads passing from plant to animal to man, up or down the scale, in an inexhaustible diversity, transiency, and recurrence of shapes. Here they had to cope with such strange concepts as karma, reincarnation, the wheel of rebirths, Nirvana.

The young world of the invaders now became unimaginably old. The small world they had brought with them began to fade into an abyss. Their thoughts turned inward. A human individual, they concluded, is but a transient mode or expression of *Atman* or Soul, of Brahman the one breather in all that breathes, the one speaker in everything that has voice, the one seer, the one hearer, the one thinker, apart from whom the individual has no reality.

It is amazing how soon Ralph Waldo Emerson entered into this, when the Bhagavad Gita and some of the Upanishads first became available in translation, and how tersely and accurately he gave expression to it in his "Brahma"—a poem, said Van Wyck Brooks, to make you gasp with its sublimity. Every line of it is from the Upanishads.

> If the red slayer think he slays,
>   Or if the slain think he is slain,
> They know not well the subtle ways
>   I keep, and pass, and turn again.
>
> Far or forgot to me is near;
>   Shadow and sunlight are the same;
> The vanished gods to me appear;
>   And one to me are shame and fame.
>
> They reckon ill who leave me out;
>   When me they fly, I am the wings;
> I am the doubter and the doubt,
>   And I the hymn the Brahmin sings.
>
> The strong gods pine for my abode.
>   And pine in vain the sacred seven;

But thou, meek lover of the good,
Find me, and turn thy back on heaven.

"Turn thy back on heaven," for Brahman is the ineffable supreme bliss. "When all the desires that dwell in the heart are cast away, then does the mortal become immortal, then he attains Brahman here."[9] And when he who has attained such bliss dies, he is welcomed in crossing over as Brahman himself. "As villagers wait with gifts for a king who is coming, saying, 'Here he comes, here he comes!' even so for him who knows this all beings wait, saying, *Here comes Brahman, here he approaches.'* "[10]

The utterly transcendent Brahman whom the mind can never reach is also immanent, the essential self of everything that exists; and so the poets sing;

Thou art the dark-blue bird,
Thou art the green parrot with red eyes.
Thou art the cloud with lightning in its womb.
Thou art the seasons and the seas,
Beginningless, omniscient, Thou from
whom all worlds are born.[11]

Man is not unique in being an incarnation of Brahman; so are all things and all creatures. But man is unique in that he may come to be aware of this, or may come to be grasped by it, enthused, although incapable of comprehending it.

To whomsoever it is not known,
  to him it is known.
To whomsoever it is known,
  he does not know.
It is not understood by those who
  understand it;
It is understood by those who do not
  understand it.[12]

After the time of the forest sages and the Upanishads came the return in India of theisms without number, along with the worship of Krishna, Rama, and other avatars of Vishnu. The Beyond had to be mediated or brought closer. To the yoga of contemplation and the yoga of works had to be added, for the human heart, the yoga of bhakti, of love and devotion. But to the thoughtful Hindu to this day the gods are but names, manifestations, of the Nameless, the Unmanifest. The quest turns inward.

The One, the controller, the inner self of all things,
Who makes the one form manifold,
To the wise who perceive him as abiding within the soul.
To them is eternal bliss.[13]

Who sees his Lord within every creature,
Deathlessly dwelling amidst the mortal,
That man sees truly.[14]

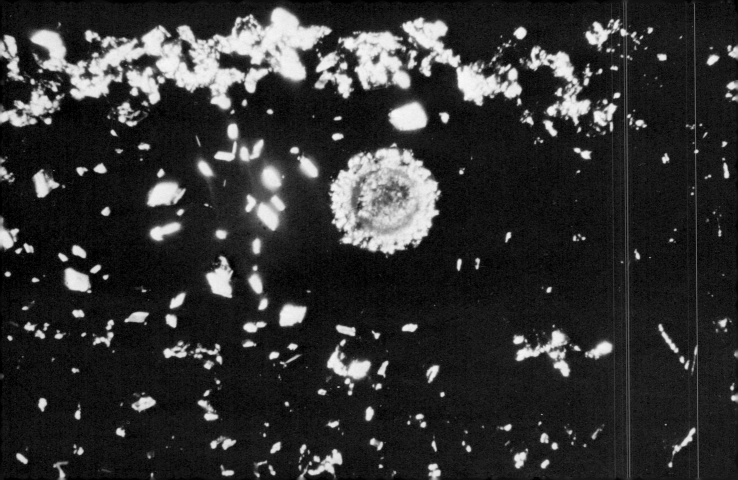

4. The Buddha: Not by Bread Alone

In early Buddhism, seen through the haze of a centuries-old tradition, the other world of mystery beyond and mystery within was mediated for the disciple through "the enlightened one," the Tathagata (He who has come), the heavenly-endowed person, the great teacher.

Of the Buddha's life we know only the bare outline. His name was Siddhartha Gautama. The son of an aristocratic Hindu chieftain of the second or warrior caste, he was brought up in princely luxury in a northern kingdom under the snows of the highest mountains in the world. One of the sutras quotes him as saying: "I had three palaces, one for the cold season, one for the hot, and one for the season of rains. Through the four rainy months, entertained by female minstrels, I did not come down from the palace." Legend has it that an overprotective father tried to keep him in or near the palace, but that he broke away, as sons do, and went out into the world on his own. There he saw for the first time the spectacle of human suffering.

In the later Buddhist scriptures the Buddha's conception and birth are accompanied with miraculous portents. The king, who wishes to have a son who will be a monarch and not a Buddha, summons sixty-four eminent sages and anxiously consults them. He is assured that if the son continues to live the household life he will become a monarch, but if he leaves the household and retires from the world, he will become a Buddha. Advised by an ascetic that the four signs which would make his son retire from the world are a decrepit old man, a diseased man, a dead man, and a monk, the king issues commands and rings the palace with guards to insure that such encounters will never take place. But the gods see to it that the four signs appear before the future Buddha by themselves taking on the semblance in turn of decrepitude, disease, death, and monkhood.

Behind all this we see a young man developing a taste for silently and anonymously escaping from the palace walls, as he begins to break free from father-domination and the life of luxury at court. We see a brooding, sensitive young genius overcome by the knowledge that beauty fades, that there is in life a falling, a fatality, so that nothing remains. "Decay is inherent in all component things." There is no escape from this, no meaning in it, no answer. The young man was suddenly old. The life smothered in luxury was suddenly and devastatingly empty.

Then one night he left the palace and his sleeping wife and child and took up the life of a wandering mendicant, exchanging his princely garb for the saffron cotton robe of a monk. At twenty-nine or thirty he was off in search of an answer. He tried various methods of meditation, and then mortification of the flesh in the company of five Hindu ascetics. Finally, reduced to skin and bones, he decided this was the way to death rather than to illumination. He strengthened himself with food, so that his mind might be active again, and then seated himself "on his throne of grass under the bo-tree" with the resolve that he would not leave the spot until he had achieved illumination. After forty-nine days he came to the answers he was seeking, and was known thereafter in the tradition as the Buddha, the Enlightened One.

In his first sermon in the deer park at Benares he brought his message to the world: the Four Noble Truths and the Eightfold Path.

The first Noble Truth is that to exist is to suffer. "Birth is ill, decay is ill, sickness is ill, death is ill."

The second is that there is a cause or an origin of suffering or ill. The cause lies in something as natural as breathing, namely, the fact that we crave or desire. Literally, we thirst.

The third is that there is a way to overcome suffering or ill. We are not doomed forever to thirst.

The fourth is the Noble Truth of the way of overcoming, which is the eightfold path. This leads on from right knowledge or understanding (of the Four Noble Truths) to right intention or resolve; then to right speech, right conduct, right means of livelihood (as necessary disciplines of that good Middle Way between indulgence and mortification, both of which weaken and enslave), on to right effort, right mindfulness, contemplation. The goal is liberation, illumination, peace—a foretaste of Nirvana.

Nirvana, literally extinction, is an end to the thirst that makes birth ill, decay ill, sickness ill, and death ill. "Tanha (craving) is the hankering after pleasure, or existence, or success. It is the germ from which springs all human misery: birth, old-age, and suffering."[1]

Nirvana has been interpreted as union with Brahman the supreme bliss, or blissful absorption into the All. But the original meaning is not to be circumvented, of extinction: extinction of desire, extinction of thirst, extinction of life, extinction of the separate self. As a Japanese proverb states it: "Asleep, you are a Buddha."

Siddhartha Gautama seems to have believed that at death the five components of the individual person fall apart, dissolve, and are not to be reassembled. "Decay is inherent in all component things." He is cited a number of times as having referred to death as "that utter passing away which leaves nothing whatever behind." How then could death be ill? And why should not death itself bring extinction of thirst and an end to all suffering, with the end to life itself? In one of the many versions of the dying Buddha's farewell, we read;

> Tathagata, composed and quiet, spake:
> "Grieve not! the time is one for joy, not sorrow;
> That for which through ages I have aimed
> I am now about to attain.
> Delivered now from the bonds of sense,
> I go to the place of never-ending rest and peace.
> I leave these things, earth, water, fire and air,
> To rest secure where neither birth nor death ever come,
> Eternally delivered there from grief.
> Oh tell me! why should I be sorrowful?"[2]

The old Dravidian doctrine of transmigration, and of being bound through life after life to the wheel of rebirths, had left its mark on Siddhartha Gautama. Certainly it was the belief and the profound conditioning of those whom he sought to help, that the way led through a wearying number of lifetimes to an eventual overcoming of Karma and release from the round of rebirths. Buddhism was nurtured among those with such feelings and beliefs, to whom Nirvana, or extinction after a long and wearisome clinging to the wheel of rebirths, was as welcome, as wholly to be longed for, as sleep to an insomniac.

Siddhartha Gautama, the Buddha, became an exalted being come down to earth to help erring mortals find the way to release.

> Know that from time to time a Tathagata
>   is born into the world,
> A fully Enlightened One, blessed and worthy,
> Abounding in wisdom and goodness. . . .
> Unsurpassed as a guide to erring mortals,
> A teacher of gods and men, a blessed Buddha.[3]

And the Buddha, who became old and died a natural death, having suffered an acute attack of indigestion, and who called his disciples around him as he lay dying and admonished them, "Be ye lamps unto yourselves; hold fast to the truth as a refuge; work out your own salvation with diligence," himself became savior, refuge, a being exalted above the gods.

> I take my refuge, Lord, in the Blessed One,
> And in the Law, and in the Brotherhood.
> May the Blessed One receive me
> From this day forth while my life lasts,
> As a disciple who has taken his refuge in Him.[4]

Siddhartha Gautama, a rare, rich, radiant person, a man of profound compassion and genius, became the Buddha sent from above to show others the way. In Mahayana the Buddha of infinite compassion and wisdom soars above the gods in stature. The boastful gods, who make great claims, are many; the Buddhas are few.

"Work out your own salvation with diligence," became the way of so-called Hinayana or Thedavara Buddhism, persisting to this day as one of the two great branches, the southern, supposedly closer to original Buddhism. Its saints or arahants are those who gain peace through the disciplines of detachment. They do not do this for others; they show others the way. Yet their earliest scriptures, as of all Buddhists, are the Tripitaka, and here the Buddha is the exalted human yet superhuman figure through whom men draw closer to the mystery within and the mystery beyond, and to a foretaste of Nirvana.

"There is, O monks, an unborn, unoriginated, uncreated, unformed. Were there not, there would be no escape from the world of the born, originated, created, formed."[5]

The Buddhist scriptures were slow in coming, and in them the earlier and later traditions are inseparably merged. We see the Buddha in an aura of the Beyond brought near, in the radiance of a person translucent to the Light of lights.

So, over the Buddha as he lay dying under twin Sala trees, an appropriately beautiful miracle takes place. "Now at that time the twin Sala trees were all one mass of bloom with flowers out of season; and all over the body of the Tathagata these dropped and sprinkled and scattered themselves, out of reverence for the successor of the Buddhas of old. And heavenly mandarava flowers too, and heavenly sandalwood powder came falling from the sky . . . and heavenly music was sounded, out of reverence for the successor of the Buddhas of old."[6]

Although the Greeks, after Alexander's conquests, brought their philosophical subtleties to the problem of how the exalted Buddha of heavenly realms became one with the human Siddhartha, such legends as that of the twin Sala trees breaking forth into unseasonable bloom are indigenous and grew as naturally as apples grow on trees.

Buddhism then, Thedavara or Mahayana, became essentially a savior-religion, its Exalted Being one who helped people overcome suffering and eventually attain bliss. Through him men were to discover and rediscover their own Buddhahood, and know that strange bliss of oneness with the beyond themselves within themselves. Eventually, they would enter Nirvana: extinction of thirst, extinction of separateness, absorption into the All.

"Those who hold nothing dear have no woe."[7]

"Hunger is the greatest ill, existence the greatest sorrow. Sure knowledge of this is Nirvana, highest bliss."[8]

"Asleep, you are a Buddha."

5. Mahayana: The Buddha's Compassionate Inconsistency

Mahayana has its own beautiful version of the Buddha's temptation as he sat on his throne of grass under the bo tree. He had attained his illumination and could now enter into the peace and bliss of Nirvana. Mara, the evil one, and the inclination of his own soul, tempted him to do so. The goal of all existence was there before him. The gate stood open. Why not enter?

"Then in the mind of the Blessed One, the thought arose, 'I have penetrated this doctrine, which is profound, difficult to perceive and to understand, exalted, unattainable by reason, known only to the wise, bringing quietude of heart. But this people, given to desire, intent upon desire, delighting in desire, will resist this knowledge to the utmost. Now if I proclaim the doctrine of quietude, extinction of desire, absence of passion, Nirvana, this would result only in frustration and weariness to me.'"

As the Blessed One ponders this matter, he becomes more and more inclined to remain quiet and not to preach the doctrine. Whereupon the great God Brahma himself becomes concerned, and comes down to plead with the Buddha.

"May the Blessed One preach the doctrine! There are beings whose mental eyes are darkened by scarcely any dust; but if they do not hear the doctrine, they cannot attain salvation. These will understand."

But the Blessed One resists. "This doctrine will be difficult to understand by the many who are lost in lust and hatred, surrounded with thick darkness."

A second time, and a third, Brahma Sahampati implores the Blessed One to preach the doctrine.

Then the Blessed One looked with the eye of a Buddha, full of compassion toward sentient beings, over the world. The Blessed One saw some whose eyes were darkened by scarcely any dust, others blinded by much dust; some sharp of intellect, and others blunted and dull; some of good disposition, some of bad; some easy to instruct, and others unteachable. . . .

And when the Blessed One, looking over the world with the eye of compassion, had seen all these, he addressed Brahma Sahampati in the following stanza:

> " 'Opened wide is the door of the Immortal
> To all who have ears to hear;
> Let them go forth with faith to meet it.
> The Dhamma sweet and good, I spake not, Brahma,
> Despairing of the weary task."

Then Brahma Sahampati understood: "The Blessed One grants my request that He should preach the doctrine."[1]

This, which has been called "the Buddha's love-filled inconsistency," is the root of Mahayana. Instead of entering into the peace and the bliss of Nirvana, Siddhartha Gautama turned back to the difficult, wearisome task of trying to show others the way. And by his act he said in effect that there is something greater than peace, namely love. Peace could wait. "Without sorrows none becomes a Buddha."

The Buddhist parable of a savior pictures one who, after a long and arduous journey through the dark forest of this world, finally comes to a veritable garden of Eden, a blissful haven of beauty and joy. Instead of entering it, as he is free to do, he turns back the long hard way he has come in order to help others toward the Eden he has found. A savior, in other words, is one who, having overcome karma, may enter heaven; but turns back instead to help others enter with him.

Such is the essential meaning of Mahayana, the Great Vehicle, or the Great Raft, big enough to carry all creatures across the sea of sorrows to the haven of Nirvana. This remarkable flowering of Buddhism took place first of all in China in the early centuries of our era, where it became the basic folk religion of China's teeming millions.

The saviors who would help fill the Great Ship of Compassion to carry all creatures eventually across the sea of sorrows, were called Bodhisattvas (on the way toward Buddhahood). These Mahayana saints took the vow never to enter Nirvana until all creatures, down to the least blade of grass, should enter with them. In other words, they chose to return to earth again and again, to remain bound to the wheel of rebirths, in order to help release others.

The prototype of all the Bodhisattvas among the Chinese was Amitabha, or O-mi-t'o Fu, who came to have the chief place in Chinese worship and devotion. His story relates that he began his career as a Buddhist monk, a wearer of the yellow robe, until finally, through the four Mahayana approaches of love, knowledge, good works, and meditation, he entered the company of the Buddhas. This was in a heaven just below Nirvana, for even a Buddha, in Mahayana, does not enter Nirvana until all can enter with him. There, in the company of the Buddhas, Amitabha took the forty-eight vows, the final one being that he would help rescue all living beings in all the different spheres of existence, and that he would keep on reentering the round of rebirths for that purpose. Then, according to the classics of the Mahayana Pure Land School, he was introduced to mortals by Gautama Buddha himself as "the merciful All-Father Amitabha."

Amitabha may be said to be the Chinese Mahayana Christ, a Christ who refuses to sit at the right hand of God the Father in heaven, but keeps returning to suffer and be crucified over and over again, until all may enter heaven with him.

The idea also of "the Christ in every man" comes to flower in Mahayana; for it was taught that if one follows the Amitabha idea to its uttermost one comes to one's own heart. There *Am* ultimately reveals himself, as known from within, the very core of one's existence, one's real self.

Mahayana has also its merciful madonna, Kuan-Yin, pictured often as carrying an infant, originally a goddess of mercy, of whom a beautiful proverb says, "The goddess of mercy has a thousand arms and needs them all." Kuan-Yin too is a Bodhisattva, born over and over again to share every lot of womankind, born into the very dregs of human society in order that there, in her work of redemption, she may undergo what the most unfortunate and degraded of women have undergone.

So, into the rigorous cause-and-effect sequence of early Buddhism, with its inescapable karma, there entered something which the Christian calls grace or the unmerited love of God. It is possible, after all, to be helped by another. It is possible even, by repeating over and over again the sacred name, with faith and as a prayer, to appropriate to one's undeserving self something of the immense store of surplus merit, of overflowing goodness, accumulated by such a Bodhisattva as Amitabha.

Said the Buddhist saint Honen, of Japan's great Bodhisattva:

Now Amida Buddha's great heart of compassion was so intent on working out a plan of salvation for men, that actually five kalpas of time slipped by without his realizing it, when finally He hit upon the best plan of all. This was to vow He would create a Pure Land to dwell in, to which He would bring the very lowest and most ignorant, who, He saw, could not attain birth there by their own exertions. He therefore decided He would go through all possible austerities Himself, however painful, through countless kalpas of time, in their stead and on their behalf. . . . Then concentrating in His own name every indefectible virtue, He would have sentient beings appropriate the same by calling upon the sacred name, promising that whenever any would from their hearts call on Him, He would remember His vow and grant them birth into His Pure Land.[2]

In the Mahayana hell, rivaling Dante's inferno in its graphic pictures of appropriate punishments, but not having *Abandon all hope* inscribed over its gateway, there is a special savior of the underworld, a compassionate Bodhisattva named Ti-ts'ang, who has made hell his special province and taken the vow never to leave it until all may leave it with him.

There are masses for the dead in Mahayana Buddhism, a rite which may have been imitated from Nestorian Christians who entered China in the early centuries of the Christian era. A dramatization in this Mahayana mass or ritual tells of a son who went down to hell to rescue his mother. As he stood by helpless to remove her or to alleviate her suffering, and as before his eyes she was about to be plunged into a burning cauldron, he offered to plunge himself into it in her place and to take upon himself the remaining full measure of her sufferings. The gods, looking down upon the scene, were moved to effect her instantaneous release, and his too.

Amitabha is addressed as follows in this Mahayana Mass for the dead:

> Thou perfect master,
> Who shinest upon all things and all men
> As gleaming moonlight plays upon a thousand
>   waters at the same time,

Thy great compassion does not pass by a
    single creature!
Steadily and quietly sails the great ship
    of compassion across the sea of sorrow.
Thou art the great physician for a sick and
    impure world,
In pity giving the invitation to the Paradise
    of the West.[3]

This doctrine of love and grace was "like a still, pure, bubbling spring, gushing out over the arid desert of legalistic systems and ascetic practices. Great and noble spirits sought its refreshment." Thousands of Mahayana saints took the vow that not in a thousand rebirths would they enter the Pure Land, the Mahayana heaven, or the Nirvana of bliss, until the whole of teeming creation, everywhere and through all cycles of time, should enter with them.

Within its context of beliefs, Mahayana was one of the noblest, if not the noblest, of all religious manifestations.

Absurd, but sublime!

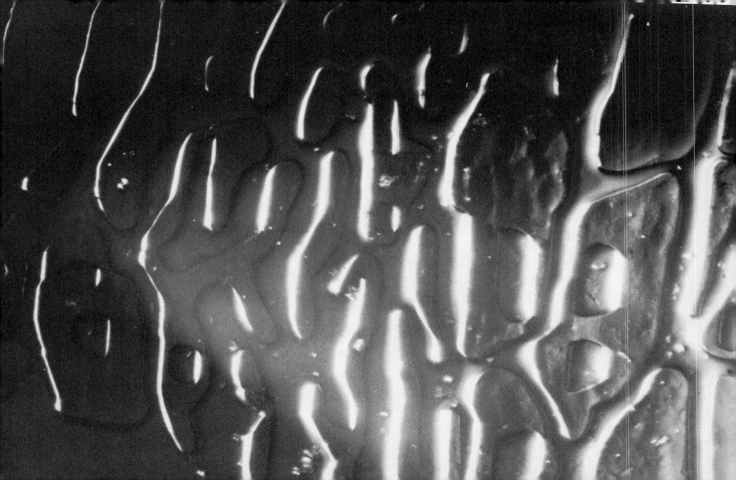

6. The Jew and the Captivity

The secret of Jewishness is the onerous burden and the sublime absurdity of being a people chosen of God. Or so it seems, but who—Jew or Gentile—will fathom what it means to be a son or a daughter of Israel?

A Jew is a guardian and transmitter of the sacred seed. With the birth of the true heir (how miraculous!) when Abraham was a hundred years old, and Sarah ninety, came the complete exclusion of Ishmael, then and ever since.

Later came another exclusion. "Esau took his wives of the daughters of Canaan." There have been many Esaus; they all sired Edomites.

"Was not Esau Jacob's brother? saith the Lord: yet I loved Jacob, but Esau I hated."[1] According to the high Calvinists, the supralapsarians, this choice was from eternity.

"But, thou, Israel, art my servant, Jacob whom I have chosen, the seed of Abraham my friend."

"And I will establish my covenant between me and these and thy seed after thee. . . ."

"Unto thy seed will I give this land."

"And in thy seed shall all the nations of the earth be blessed."

St. Paul, intensely a Jew, yet took the radical step of exalting faith above lineal descent in his profound concern that Gentile believers in Messiah Jesus should be legitimate children of Abraham, by faith, and therefore heirs of the promise.

To be a Jew, further, meant being true to the covenant made with Abraham and later with Moses and his people at Sinai. The covenant is with a people, and with the individual only as responsible to a people and a people's God. (In Israel today there are those who say that only an Israeli can be a real Jew.)

In Psalm 73, where the theme is the mystery of prosperous wickedness, the solution is found in belonging to a people and so also drawing near to a people's God, the Eternal One. This great poem could well have been written by one who was distressed by the arrogant wealthy at home; but if written in exile, as many of the Psalms were, the mystery may have been the prosperity of the godless conquerors in contrast to the ghetto existence of the people of God.

> Therefore his people return hither;
> And waters of a full cup are wrung out of them.
> And they say, How doth God know?

And is there knowledge in the Most High?
Behold, these are the wicked;
And, being always at ease, they increase in riches.

The poet, who was "envious of the arrogant" and complained, "Surely in vain have I cleansed my heart," comes back to his opening line, "Surely God is good to Israel," in the realization that in his envy he has been unfaithful to his people and to his people's God. "Behold, I have dealt treacherously with the generation of thy children."

Then he goes into the sanctuary, into that deeper level of his existence where the wicked, even though "They are not in trouble as other men," are bereft of what he has, the refuge of belonging to "the generation of thy children" and thus to the Father of all. In the poet's beautiful "nevertheless I am continually with thee," he does not contrast himself as an individual with other individuals, nor as a good man with others who are bad. He nestles into the sacred community and its sanctuary and thus draws close to God, who now becomes the strength of his heart and his portion for ever.

This poet, like many another since, became again a Jew, that is, one of a holy seed set apart, one of a people who would dissolve as a people without their *I am that I am* who went with them from place to place when they were nomads, with them into Babylonian exile, with them into the Diaspora, with them—beyond all reason or belief —into the gas chambers.

After Dachau, after Belsen and Buchenwald, many a Jew has asked in utter anguish,

"How can there be a Judaism? Three out of four Jews in Europe, two out of five in the whole world, dead! How can we who survive return again to a love of our cruel God?"

But this God "who dwells in the praises of his people" is cruel only as human beings are cruel, loving only as human beings are loving. He is a hidden God, a *deus abscon-ditus*, when men turn from him to willfulness, irresponsibility, blind passion; a God manifest when men become his sons through being brothers of their brothers. Reason cannot find such a God. He is not the God of the philosophers, but the God of Abraham, of Isaac, and of Jacob. Through belief in him, the Incredible One, the Jewish community enters and reenters into a life-affirming humanism and a cosmic at-homeness. By saying Yes to this God who dwells in their praises, the Jews say Yes to life, Yes to each other, Yes to their impossible world.

How human is this God of Israel!

To love him, for many a pious Jew, is to argue with him. Or even to accuse him.

There is a Hasidic story of a tailor who argued with God on Yom Kippur.

"You wish me to repent of my sins, but I have committed only minor offences, like keeping bits of leftover cloth, or eating with unwashed hands in a non-Jewish home where I was working.

"But You, O Lord, have committed grievous sins, like taking away babies from their mothers, or mothers from their babies. So let us be quits: You forgive me, and I will forgive You."

His rabbi, to whom he had recounted this, said: "Why did you let God off so easily? You might have forced him to redeem all Israel."

As one feels sorry for Hosea, attached with absurd unbreakable bonds of love to a woman who despises him and leaves him, so one feels sorry for Yahveh, in love similarly with an indifferent people. He is the most frustrated and abused character in the Hebrew Bible, for whom nothing ever turns out right.

Brother Antoninus has a searing poem, "A Frost Lay White on California," in which this God is likened to a dog, mistreated again and again, yet coming back to lick the foot that kicks him; also to a slave who comes when he is called, and begs only for the sheerest recognition that he does exist.[2]

On the other hand, how about this God and his promises? The Jews, according to their own wry comment on their own history, should have a special holiday to commemorate God's broken promises.

The theme of the Torah, beside that of tracing the true descent of the people of God, is that of a land grant to the patriarchs. This land, although they had but grazing rights to a parcel of it, Jacob and his sons could not take with them to Egypt. It was retaken by violence centuries later, as our forefathers in America took the land from the Indians. After a few brief centuries the northern kingdom of Israel was destroyed, never to rise again from its ashes. Judah, then captive to Babylon, was liberated by the Persians to be briefly an independent country again, then a province within the Hellenic and Roman empires, finally destroyed by Rome and dispersed through the nearly two thousand years of the Diaspora.

Yet these scattered Jews remained somehow a people, "the people of the Book," the people of lost identity without their Book, the people of a profound need to fulfill themselves in being a people, yearning to return to the land where they could be a people. For what is a people without a land, a bit of Mother Earth to be attached to and nourished by, where it can realize its own uniqueness and enjoy its own freedom?

The people protected themselves against assimilation with "the fence of the law," and Christians helped them by pushing them behind walls, yet it does seem a miracle beyond the age of miracles that the Jews, from Yemen to Siberia, from Africa and Europe to the New World, should have remained Jews and retained the sense of being a people. Even the harassed Marranos of Spain, suspected of being Jews wearing protective Christian masks, somehow still belonged to the people, as did those Sabbatians who followed the example of Sabbatai Zevi in converting to Islam—for this, in their view, was a necessary tragic moment in the Messiah's destiny. As the exile draws to a close, the Messiah himself must be exiled to atone for Israel's sins. So it is said too, in the Zohar, that God himself is in exile and will not enter the heavenly Jerusalem until his people enter Jerusalem here on earth.

All through the earlier centuries, of a people divided into two kingdoms, north and south, and divided in their worship of Yahveh and the local Baals, the prophets and idealists dreamed of a Messiah, a just and truly anointed king who would lead his people into true worship and right ways under the covenant of Sinai. The people have no Messiah, said one of the earlier prophets, because they are not yet fit to receive one. During the centuries of exile, of brief and precarious independent existence and then of foreign domination, the life of the people became one great longing for messianic deliverance. And all through the later centuries of exile and dispersion, scattered Israel was one deep sigh, one unutterable yearning, one long prayer for the return to Zion and the coming of the messianic age.

The vision had been uttered by Isaiah, and this, said H. G. Wells, was the first enunciation in the West of the world-state idea—an enthusiastic misinterpretation, for what was depicted was not a world-state but a community of nations coming to Zion to learn from the Torah entrusted to the people of Israel, whose mission it was to bring this light to the world.

> And it shall come to pass in the latter days
> that the mountain of the Lord's house
> shall be established as the loftiest of mountains,
> and shall be exalted above the hills,
> and all the nations shall flow unto it.
> And many peoples shall come, and say,
> Come, let us go up to the mountain of the Lord,
>   to the house of the God of Jacob,
> that he may teach us his ways
> and that we may walk in his paths.
> For out of Zion shall go forth the law,
> and the word of the Lord from Jerusalem.
> He shall judge between the nations,

and shall reprove many peoples;
and they shall beat their swords into plowshares
and their spears into pruning hooks;
nation shall not lift up sword against nation,
neither shall they learn war any more.[3]

This ideal, which soars in Habakkuk to "the earth shall be filled with the knowledge of the glory of God, as the waters cover the sea," is the burden of what it means, religiously, to be a Jew.

Now that there is again a visible Zion, will the hidden Zion, which the prophets demanded be made a lived and open reality, begin to emerge there?

Will there be a new Jerusalem, radiating its truth and righteousness across the whole world?

This seems too much to expect, humanly.

It seems too much also, in reason or experience, to expect or hope that "in the Lord shall all the seed of Israel be justified, and shall glory."

Yet this is the unique Jewish approach to the Ineffable, the Imageless, the Eternal: that in ways utterly beyond fathoming he works in and through them and in and through history. Or, in a more intimate sense, through *their* history. We come closer to its reality in the *Sh'ma:* "Hear, O Israel, the Lord your God is one." Here it is not said, "Hear, everyone or all people, the Lord, the God, is one," but "Hear, O Israel, community of YHVH, the Lord *your* God is one."

7. Zarathustra: Maker of the West

This side the abyss of endless space there were always myriads of stars. And this side of the infinitely infinite Infinite there were hosts of angels and archangels, and myriads of their dark fallen counterparts.

The epiphany of Jesus in the Gospel according to St. Mark is that he has power over the invisible Adversary. After his baptism and temptation by Satan in the wilderness he goes to Galilee, where, walking by the sea, he calls the fishermen Simon and Andrew his brother, and James and John the sons of Zebedee, to be his disciples. "Come with me, and I will make you fishers of men." Then in Capernaum he goes into the synagogue to teach.

"And there was in their synagogue a man with an unclean spirit; and he cried out, saying, Let us alone; what have we to do with thee, thou Jesus of Nazareth? art thou come to destroy us? I know thee who thou art, the Holy One of God.

"And Jesus rebuked him, saying, Hold thy peace, and come out of him. And when the unclean spirit had torn him, and cried with a loud voice, he came out of him."[1]

The people were amazed, and wondered by what authority he had power even over the unclean spirits. "And immediately his fame spread throughout all the region round about Galilee."

Soon thereafter "all the city" was gathered together at the door of Simon's house, where he had cured Simon's wife's mother of a fever. "And he healed many that were sick of divers diseases, and cast out many devils; and suffered not the devils to speak, because they knew him."

Again and again, in this earliest of the canonical Gospels, Jesus manifests his power over the Adversary by casting out devils, a whole legion of them from one man in the country of the Gadarenes.

To understand this strange atmosphere into which Christianity was born, it is necessary to have a look at what happened centuries earlier in Persia, through a remarkable man named Zarathustra.

The religion he founded is called Zoroastrianism. The great Persian kings one reads about in the Bible were Zoroastrians. Persia had its time of far-flung empire, during and after which Iranian religion and culture became a dominant influence throughout the Near East. Judaism, Christianity, and Islam would not be quite what they are today if this prophet called Zarathustra or Zoroaster had never lived. The dualism, the teeming demonic world of the Essenes and the early Christians, the somber cast of St. Augustine's thought, the demonology of the Middle Ages, Calvin's paradoxically envigorating effect, all owe something to the prophet Zarathustra.

The Persians, Indo-Europeans whose basic language was Sanskrit, were of the same tide that pushed and fought its way down into India. They shared the same cultus of many gods and goddesses, bloody sacrifices, holy intoxication from a plant juice called Soma. There was a class of warriors and chieftains who fought and ruled, a class of priests who conducted rites and sacrifices, and a third class which seems to have existed mainly to serve the other two. Among the latter were herdsmen trying to settle down to a peaceful and productive existence, who were often victimized by roving rapacious chieftains and their warriors, lusting to fight and unacquainted with work. After raiding and plundering the herdsmen's premises, they rode off with stolen cattle for their feasts and sacrifices.

Zoroastrianism, it has been said, is the only historic religion which originated in answer to the cry of suffering animals. This is dramatized in the Gathas, where the Lord who is the Creator of Cattle hears the supplication of kine given over to senseless slaughter. The soul of the cattle wails aloud, and in response to the lament of the Ox-soul Zarathustra is called to be a prophet and is given the gift of inspired speech.

Like the Hebrew prophets, Zarathustra was intervening in behalf of the oppressed, and expressing also his opposition to the cult of animal sacrifice.

With the help of certain members of the class he was opposing, Zarathustra carried out during his lifetime a remarkable reformation. There was retrogression after he died, when the priestly class, the Magi, waxed stronger and stronger. Yet the peculiar monotheism of Zarathustra, which set the one God of light with all his angels over against the powers of darkness was to live after him and make its way westward to Palestine, to Rome, to Geneva, and to the farthest outposts of Christendom.

This one God Zarathustra addressed as Ahura, which means "Lord" and was a title given to both gods and men, like the Hebrew *Adon* and the Greek *Kyrios.* He addressed him also as Mazdah, meaning the All-Wise. How sweeping Zarathustra's attempted reform was may be seen in the fact that personified ethical and spiritual states or attributes were substituted for the anthropomorphic gods and goddesses. The attendant spirits of Ahura Mazdah were Good Thought, Order, Desired Dominion, Devotion, Well-Being, Immortality. "Good Thoughts" was the first angel of God! The All-Wise Lord was spoken of often as "the Father of the Good Mind."

Over against this first angel of God, however, was his dark counterpart, the Evil Spirit, Ahriman, the Father of the Lie. The Daeva or gods of the old religion became the devils of the disciples of Zarathustra.

"Now the two primal Spirits, who revealed themselves as Twins, are what is Good and what is Bad in thought and word and action. And between these two the wise choose aright, the foolish not so."[2]

"I will tell of the two spirits in the beginning of the world, the holy of whom spake thus to the hostile: 'Neither our thoughts, nor our doctrines, nor our purposes, nor our convictions, nor our words, nor our works, nor our selves, nor our souls agree.' "[3]

In the Manual of Discipline of the Essene Community at Qumran, we read:

"God, who created man to rule the world, appointed for him two spirits after whose direction he was to walk until the final Judgment. They are the spirits of truth and of perversity.

"The origin of the one is the Fountain of Light, of the other, the Wellspring of Darkness. All who practice righteousness are under the dominion of the Prince of Lights, and walk in his ways; but the willfully wrong are under the dominion of the Angel of Darkness, and walk in his ways."[4]

We read further that God has set an eternal enmity between these two, and that until the final age neither the one nor the other shall prevail.

We read of a war between the Sons of Light and the Sons of Darkness, and of the final victory "when wrong will depart before right, as darkness disappears before light."

The cosmos, in Zoroastrianism, is the scene of a great war between the powers of light and the powers of darkness. Man is to be no mere passive spectator, but a combatant in the thick of the fight. "He that is not for us is against us." Every man by his own choice is arrayed under the one banner or the other. Salvation is to be sought, in Zarathustra's doctrine, not by fleeing from this world, but by ranging oneself on the side of the angels and helping them to fight their battle for the sake of the right.

Zoroastrianism is Christianity's godfather. Ideas of a life after death and a resurrection of the body, of hosts of angels and devils in combat and of an Armageddon to come, were derived directly from Zoroastrian teachings, as were the ideas of a supernatural savior, an end of this world by fire from heaven, a final judgment, and heaven and hell. St. Paul's writings have a strong tincture of Zoroastrianism: "For our fight is not against human foes, but against cosmic powers, against the authorities and potentates of this dark world, against the superhuman forces of evil in the heavens."[5]

But the fight was also against the demonic in the human, and in this contest Zarathustra took the vigorous down-to-earth stance of a real maker of the West.

"He who sows corn sows righteousness: he makes the religion of Mazdah walk."

Irrigation is called "showing a beautiful path to the waters."

Again and again in the Zendavesta the prophet asks Ahura Mazdah who rejoices the world with greatest joy, and the answer in effect is always: "He who makes two blades of grass grow where one grew before." The earth feels most happy where there is most increase of flocks and herds, "where land untilled wants a good husbandman, like a well-shaped maiden who has long gone childless and wants a good mate." The earth rejoices "where one of the faithful erects a house, waters ground that is dry or drains a swamp,—where cattle thrive, virtue thrives, fodder thrives, women and children thrive, fire thrives, and every blessing of life thrives."

Arnold Toynbee, in his "Litany of Faiths," wherein he addresses all the great saviors, saints, founders and avatars of high religion, invokes Zarathustra as follows: "Valiant Zarathustra, breathe thy spirit into the Church Militant here on earth."[6] When Christianity at its this-worldly best was essentially a fighting, public-spirited religion, optimistic, believing in the possibility of change for the better and striving for it, we see the spirit of valiant Zarathustra at work. Yet the spirit of the "Church Militant" and of "He that is not for us is against us" has its dangers, making Western religions the most intolerant of all.

In a Thedavara catechism, published in translation "in the year 2438 after the entering into Nirvana of the Buddha," there is a question, number 143: "What are the relations of Buddhism to other believers?" the answer reads: "It commands us to look upon all men as our brothers, without distinction of race, nationality or creed; to respect the convictions of men of other beliefs and to be careful to avoid religious controversy. The Buddhist doctrine is imbued with the purest spirit of perfect toleration; nowhere and at no time has blood been shed for its diffusion. Never has it, after acquiring ascendency, persecuted or oppressed other believers."[7]

"There can never be a war of Buddhism," it is said. "No ravished country has ever born witness of the followers of Buddha."

Whether or not this is wholly true, nothing approximating such a claim could be made by the religions of the West.

St. Augustine, as a convert to Manichaeanism, was for ten years under the spell of that ultimate or extreme dualism whose founder was a Persian named Mani, born in 215 A.D. This religious innovator, whose inheritance was Zoroastrian, worked out a myth of his own in which the realms of light and darkness, good and evil, were an eternal dualism of opposites.

His myth tells us that for a long time the two kingdoms coexisted without intermingling. Then Satan made war on the kingdom of light, and God begat Primal Man to be his champion and defender. But Primal Man was vanquished and thrown into captivity. God himself then took the field, routed evil, and released the captive. Meanwhile a not easily reparable confusion of the two kingdoms had been wrought. Seeds of darkness had been scattered widely in the soil of light, and innumerable seeds of light sown deeply in the darkness. These elements must be sorted out and returned to their own. On earth, man is the subject of this peculiar drama of division. He is dominated by Satan, who placed in his dark substance all the particles of light he could steal, so that he could control them. Man is therefore a house divided against itself. Demons seek to abet the darkness in him by teaching him false religions; and certain activities, like sexual pleasure, eating flesh, taking life, are victories of darkness. The light in man is liberated by the teachings of the true prophets: Adam, Noah, Abraham, Zarathustra, Buddha, Christ, Paul, and Mani himself. When all the particles of light are liberated, the kingdom of light will be perfected. But the kingdom of darkness will not be annulled. It remains a part of reality. The two eternal kingdoms will again be separate and distinct.

(So in Judaism there is the myth of the divine sparks of holiness, *mitzotzot*, which fell at the time of Adam's sin into the impure realm of *kelipot*.)

The chief attraction of Manichaeanism for St. Augustine was that its dualism could furnish an adequate or rational explanation of sin. For this reason also Manichaeanism, whether or not so called, shows up here and there throughout the history of Christianity. It was the great heretical cry of the Middle Ages, when a number of sects were influenced by its ideas.

> I form the light, and create darkness:
> I make peace, and create evil:
> I am the Lord, that doeth all these things.[8]

Texts such as this one, from Second Isaiah, are hard to accept. Reason cannot reconcile, nor can the heart, the fact of evil with the goodness of an omnipotent and sovereign deity. One way out is to accept the idea that there is a ultimate principle of evil in the world over against an ultimate principle of good. Another, rather prevalent not long ago, is to posit a finite, struggling, suffering God.

It is said that St. Augustine joined the Manichaeans because of sin and left them because of astronomy. The regular motion of the stars, mathematical, predictable and harmonious, made him question the idea of a basic dualism or of demonic creation.

Whether or not the ultimate is addressed as Thou, "the eternal Thou who cannot be expressed but only addressed," every religion is a theodicy, a "justification of God," in the attempt to find meaning in suffering or evil and in trying to give inner resources to meet the crises of suffering and death.

Experience has shown that there is little, if any, solace in the various forms of futurism —a heaven beyond this life, Nirvana at the end of a long succession of rebirths, a secular utopia at the end of a class struggle. Some far-off Eden, or a ghostly perfection in some spirit world beyond this one, changes nothing and can compensate for nothing that precedes it. Men have found solace rather, if they have found it at all, in the nowness of participating in Being, in the Christhood or Buddhahood within, in the soul's ongoing as a you-in-others, in the human spirit's recognition of the glory of the One breaking through.

Sisyphus rolling the stone uphill only to have it roll down again may be a valid symbol of man and his outward achievements. But when he turns to take up the task once more, and asserts his dignity over against indignity and frustration, then something within him transcends the given situation; as when, accepting the fact of diminishment and death he yet struggles against them; or, knowing that evil cannot be entirely of his own making, he accepts his share of responsibility for it, and with Zarathustra and St. Paul puts on the armor of God to fight with the angels.

8. Christianity of No Avail

In Origen's *Reply to Celsus* he cites his opponent so generously and conscientiously that we have a fairly accurate and comprehensive idea of what Celsus' objections were to the new cult called Christianity. Celsus objected first of all to Christian intolerance. Zeus, Jupiter, Apollo, Jehovah, et cetera, are but names. Why try to adopt and exalt one to the exclusion of all the others? Christians, he thinks, are guilty of name-worship and name-magic. Such Christian beliefs as the virgin birth of a god-man, the miracles, the resurrection, were subjected to the acute rational scrutiny of a cultivated second-century Roman and shown to be absurd and therefore untenable, to any rationalist then or since. Celsus, the Stoic, spoke the language of the prevailing secularism of our time. Origen, the believer, the enthusiast, spoke the language of religion.

Although Origen's mixture of early Christianity and Neoplatonism was strictly of its time, his affirmation as he was led away to imprisonment and torture was timeless: "Our confidence is in him who said, 'Be of good cheer, I have overcome the world.' "

The convincing Christian argument against Celsus and against Rome was not philosophic. Nor was it the ethics Christianity brought with it from Judaism, making it superior to Mithraism and other mysteries. The nobler Roman could and did respect the ethics of Deuteronomy and the prophets. The convincing Christian argument was that it made sons of God of Rome's slaves and disinherited, of whom there were too many, and that it drew these lowly ones, who were as dust under the feet of the proud, into communities of equality and of caring for one another.

When St. Augustine said, "No one, indeed, believes anything, unless he previously knows it to be believable," the dew of Christianity's morning freshness was beginning to evaporate. The great theological controversies of Nicaea and Chalcedon had intervened, in the effort to make plausible the miraculously and gloriously implausible.

Tertullian in the third century was already weakening, in a human and very natural desire for plausibility, when he said defiantly, *Certum est quia impossibile est.*

In early Christianity remote and majestic transcendence was brought near in the person of Jesus the Messiah. He had "descended into hell," had conquered death and the kingdom of darkness ruled over by Satan. Although Satan and his hosts would not be cast into the pit until the imminent Second Coming, redemption had been accomplished—was present in the world now and available to all believing acceptance.

The early Christians did try to prove from the Scriptures that this was fulfillment of prophecy. But mostly they sang it; they joyfully proclaimed it. This thing had happened "in the fullness of time," and theirs, as witnesses, was the supreme privilege of spreading the Good News.

So in St. Luke it was sung by an angel chorus to shepherds watching their flocks at night, to be heard by countless shepherds since, when for them too the heavens opened.

Even after three or four generations, in the more Gnostic Fourth Gospel, it still sings, in its opening hymn, of light shining in darkness, of the Word made flesh and dwelling among us.

> And we beheld his glory,
>   the glory as of the only begotten of the Father,
> full of grace and truth.

It sings also in the announcement that the Wholly Other, the remote and sovereign transcendence, is a God who cares.

"For God so loved the world, that he gave his only begotten Son, that whosoever believeth in him should not perish, but have everlasting life."

Compare this with the language of the Athanasian Creed, *Quicumque vult*, composed at some unknown date under Augustinian influence.

> Now the catholic faith is this; that we worship one God in a Trinity, and the Trinity in a Unity;
> Neither confounding the persons, nor dividing the substance [et cetera, to the conclusion of the first section] . . . "Let him therefore that would be saved think thus of the Trinity."

Here were sown the dragon's teeth of future Inquisitions, of search and destroy missions against heretics.

The second section goes on to explicate the incarnation sung in St. John's opening hymn, and the entire formulation, which tries to make it all cut and dried and rational, succeeds in making it completely absurd.

To be saved by right knowledge, "think thus of the Trinity," was a Greek import into Christianity, like the Socratic Jesus who is cited as saying, "Ye shall know the truth, and the truth shall make you free." This text, from the eighth chapter of St. John, is seldom quoted in full: "If ye continue in my word, then are ye my disciples indeed; and ye shall know the truth, and the truth shall make you free." This freedom, as the context makes clear, is freedom from bondage to sin. In other words, this is a living, developing, experiential truth, learned through continuing in discipleship; not the rational truth with a capital *T* of the creeds and the catechisms.

The St. Augustine who said rapturously, "Too late came I to love thee, O thou beauty so ancient yet so fresh, yea too late came I to love thee; and, behold, thou wert within me, and I out of myself, where I made search for thee," also tried to make the Good News rationally and philosophically acceptable. This was natural, inevitable. The church, as an institution and as a community, had to be pedagogical as well as missionary, a house of instruction as well as a house of worship. St. Thomas Aquinas did a monumental work of putting it all together, theologically, philosophically, in an effort to show that nothing in revelation is contrary to reason. St. Thomas' *Summa theologica* was never finished. Returning to his cell from the celebration of Mass on December 6 in the year 1273, he said; "All that I have written seems to me nothing but straw—compared with what I have seen and what has been revealed to me."

Paul Tillich, in our time, tried to correlate Christian theology and tradition systematically with philosophic truth. But Paul Tillich the preacher is more convincing than Paul Tillich the philosopher-theologian; his sermons are nearly as good to read as they were to listen to—alive, passionate, communicative, out of the depths and the rich experience of a rare, courageous, gifted person.

Entire plausibility is probably unachievable, and if it were, it would be something finished and dead, whether in science, religion, or poetry. But there is always the convincingness of discovery, revelation, apocalypse, direct communication, mutual confirmation, inward music, or being struck down and overwhelmed like St. Paul.

Christianity, out of Hebrew, Iranian, and Greek antecendents, but with fresh inspiration and a grand energy of conviction, announced in a unique fashion to those who would listen the primacy of the person, the inalienable dignity of every soul fashioned in the image of God.

So Boris Pasternak, in Doctor Zhivago, after describing Rome as "a flea market of borrowed gods and conquered peoples," says: "And then, into this tasteless heap of gold and marble, He came, light and clothed in an aura, emphatically human, deliberately provincial, Galilean, and at that moment gods and nations ceased to be and man came into being—man the carpenter, man the plowman, man the shepherd with his flock of sheep at sunset, man who does not sound in the least proud, man thankfully celebrated in all the cradle songs of mothers and in all the picture galleries the world over."[1]

Not masses, not crowds crammed into passages of the Coliseum and all wretched, but in the kingdom of heaven individual souls, persons equal before God.

In the kingdom of heaven all men are equal, early or late laborers in the vineyard, Jew or Gentile, publican or Pharisee, the prodigal younger son who returns or the dutiful elder son who never leaves. To show his disciples what the kingdom of heaven is like Jesus calls a little child and sets him in their midst, or he performs the parabolic action of receiving them as guests, washing their feet and serving them at table.

St. Paul, who argumentatively tried to make belief in the Messiah who has come plausible to his fellow Jews, yet breaks out again and again into ecstatic prose, as from an inward music, about the equality of all believers.

To the church in Galatia, where the uncircumcised were being shouldered out, he exclaims wrathfully, "O foolish Galatians, who hath bewitched you, that ye should not obey the truth, before whose eyes Jesus Christ hath been evidently set forth, crucified among you?"

He then begins to expound; but soon breaks out into a ringing declaration of the kind of equality in the kingdom of heaven taught so beautifully in the parables of Jesus, to be extended now to all who come in.

"For ye are all the children of God by faith in the Lord Christ.

"For as many of you as have been baptized into Christ have put on Christ.

"There is neither Jew nor Greek, there is neither bond nor free, there is neither male or female: for ye are all one in Christ Jesus.

"And if ye be Christ's, then are ye Abraham's seed, and heirs according to the promise."[2]

St. Paul was a decisive factor in breaking down the distinction between Jew and Gentile, so that genuine communication and community, sitting at table together, became possible to them and thus also a Christianity which could be an overleaper of barriers.

He made other inestimable contributions. The first was his "Christ mysticism"—that one may suffer and die and be resurrected with Christ, and thus enter into that new creation, that new state of being which Christ has already achieved for his disciples and which, in all its fullness, will be entered into in the time to come.

This "Christ mysticism," as Dr. Albert Schweitzer pointed out,[3] was capable of outlasting its eschatological setting, which soon faded. It was capable of being experienced anew, in other times and other settings; for this sense of being in living connection with a greater than self ("Yet not I live, but Christ liveth in me") is a universal reality of religion, although always concretely and uniquely experienced in differing contexts, and always a mystery.

Another great contribution was St. Paul's superb expression and courageous example of love as the bond of fellowship. Paul was citing one of the great things of his Jewish inheritance when he spoke of love as the fulfillment of the law. Yet, having caught the inspiration of this from Jesus through Peter and other witnesses, he broadened the content and enriched the meaning.

"Love edifieth," he said. That is, love itself teaches, as no Torah or instruction, without love, can teach.

"Love is the bond of perfectness," as in the King James translation; or in the New English Bible: "To crown all, there must be love, to bind all together and complete the whole."[4] Love, the highest spiritual grace of rejoicing in the good of others, can bind together in one community like and unlike, Jew and Gentile, Greek and Roman, rich and poor, high and low.

St. Paul, who valued mystical rapture, prophecy, healing, and other gifts of the spirit, valued even more highly "this most excellent way," of which he writes so beautifully in 1 Corinthians 13, "the church's first hymn and only deathless Athanasian Creed."

Paul Tillich adopts and reexpresses in his own way this "Christ mysticism" of St. Paul in a sermon entitled "The New Being." He takes his text from St. Paul: "For neither circumcision counts for anything nor uncircumcision, but a new creature."[5] Under circumcision Dr. Tillich subsumes all the analogous rites and forms, all the doctrines, sacraments, institutions of any or all cults and churches, in contrast to which, as uncircumcision, he cites the secularization which is spreading today all over the world. Both are nothing, of no importance, he says, if the ultimate question is asked—"the question of a New Reality."

"The New Being, the newness of life which has appeared and in which we may participate—this should be our infinite passion. . . . In comparison with it everything else, even religion or non-religion, even Christianity or non-Christianity, matters very little—and ultimately nothing."[6]

In "the new being" the fear and awe with which religions begin are transmuted into reverence and love, without which all religions are empty vessels.

Christianity, like any other historic faith, has taken on much and undergone strange transformations down through the centuries. But without reverence and the kind of love that flowers from it—and these are in persons, not in institutions—it is of no importance, of no avail.

And so we may say with Paul Tillich, taking delight in his paradoxical way of saying it, that to be a Christian is to know that Christianity is an empty vessel.

"It is the greatness of Christianity that it can see how small it is. The importance of being a Christian is that one can stand the insight that it is of no importance. It is the spiritual power of religion that he who is religious can fearlessly look at the vanity of religion. It is the maturest fruit of Christian understanding to understand that Christianity, as such, is of no avail."[7]

9. Some Beautiful Superstitions

Hear the voice of the Bard,
Who present, past and future sees;
Whose ears have heard
The Holy Word
That walked among the ancient trees.

"A man bears beliefs as a tree bears apples," said Emerson. Their classification into various pigeonholes are familiar enough: preanimism, animism, totemism, polytheism, henotheism, the various theisms. Religion was concerned with relation to, and somehow coping with, whatever was perceived to be a mystery. What men and gods did in the morning of time was often cruel, bestial, immoral; but this was by no means ever the whole picture.

"We are constantly showing a lack of understanding, appreciation, and admiration of *paganism*," wrote the Dutch theologian Kornelis H. Miskotte. "To be contemptuous of paganism is simply to be contemptuous of man. . . . We must open our eyes and see the absurdity of the associations that have attached themselves to the word 'paganism' as we have been using it. Paganism is not atheism; on the contrary, it is a very strong, vital faith. . . . Paganism is not something antiquated; on the contrary, it is the everlasting ferment of human life."[1]

For those who are willing to see, a few great revelatory themes are to be found in the mythological tales and beliefs of the past, with all their amazing diversity and inventiveness. One could call these beliefs and attitudes from which revelations shine forth, "beautiful superstitions"—where "superstition" is taken to be an original standing still in fear and awe and amazement, without which there would have been no religion on this planet, no emergence of the human.

Awe and dread and fearful wonder, a new kind of feeling among the earth's inhabitants, once troubled some strange, shambling, upright creature, and there a man was born. The "sense of the numinous" was the original superstition; hence the sudden and overwhelming recognition of the power and the glory of the immense otherness. "Be still, and know that I am God."

In "animistic" times, when great sky-spirits carried the lanterns of the stars and drove the fiery chariot of the sun, there were "spirits" also in men and in all living creatures, spirits in stones, trees, and running waters. It was the spirit of a tree that made it put forth leaf and flower and fruit. In this revelatory, beautiful superstition there was everywhere and in all things a personal otherness. It was a world of *thou* and not of *it*. And for that very reason it was a completely interrelated world, a world most entirely and deeply akin to its human inhabitants. Man had none of that sense of separateness, of aloof distinctness, of being a lonely pilgrim wandering in alienation from the things and creatures of this world. He could dance to the rhythm of life and the seasons and the great world around him, and feel at-one-ment with them.

The ungodding of nature, emptying the world of its divine content, had not yet taken place. Mountains were still awesome; the God of glory still thundered.

Totemism was one expression of this divinity-in-nature superstition. "The animal divinity is eaten and is the savior of the tribe." There is something sacred, therefore, about a food animal. Hence stringent taboo against senseless slaughter for the sake of slaughter; against hunting (although dwindling stocks had to be rationed) in the Lenten season when spring pregnancies brought new offspring; and, at all times, against killing and partaking without sharing. It was his spirit or lifeblood, something sacred, that the divine animal poured forth so that other life might live. Life lives by the sacrifice of other life, as modern urban man tends to forget. "Take, eat, this is my body, broken for you."

The poor ignorant savage even apologized to a tree for having to cut it down and had sacred groves and woods he left standing—homes of the gods or of his fellow creatures —whereas his successor, who ungodded nature, ravages the heights and brings floods and dustbowls into the once fertile lowlands. Or worse, defoliates to facilitate hunting down his brother man.

In the "vegetation myth" a like reverent consideration is extended to plant life. Here, too, the divinity is eaten and is the savior of the tribe—a divinity who dies and is resurrected annually in order that men and other creatures may live.

"Our people eat quite gently," said Popovi Da, noted pueblo potter of New Mexico, "recognizing with inner feelings that the corn or the squash were at one time growing, cared for, each a plant alive, now prepared to become a part of us, of our bodies, of our minds, quite sacred."[2]

Popovi Da's less tender-minded and more materialistic brother thinks of "the corn that dies and rises again to be man's savior" as a mere commodity, perhaps, or a stock-market quotation. He may even feel free to poison it, or make chemically sterile the ground that grows it, lest the men, women, and children who are "the enemy" be fed.

Associated with the vegetation myth in many lands are upright stones, so found or uptilted by men, which still stand in some places after thousands of years. They were dedicated to, or marked the place of, the local gods and goddesses of the land, around which swirled the fertility cults of dawning agricultural civilizations. Here were two superstitions. One, that the coupling of the local god and goddess made possible the fertility of crops and herds—which had the merit at least of acknowledging that life, fertility, are derivative and that men are not makers but transmitters of life. The other superstition was that the land belonged to the local god or Baal, which would seem to be a sounder idea than that it does or can belong to the evanescent individual. Land was a community, not of men only but of plants and animals, domestic and wild.

The pueblo Indians thought of land as such a community. "We believe we are the first conservationists," said Popovi Da. "We do not destroy or disturb the harmony of nature. To us this is beauty. We care for and husband our environment, trying to be all-forebearing like mother earth. And this gives us a union with all existence, all the creatures that live in the world."[3]

The beautiful superstition that the natural powers are divine should flower, not into contempt for things, nor just exploitation of things, but into reverence for life and the potential of life; and into the spirit of St. Francis of Assisi's Canticle of the Creatures, where seeing that natural powers are less than God does not empty them of God, and where God is not loved over against the creation, but rather in and through the creation.

Democracy's superstition about man, "that all men are born equal and endowed by their Creator with certain inalienable rights," goes back to that same old animism. This is the curious or the beautiful superstition that man has a soul. An immortal person within, the size of a thumb! There are some interesting passages about this in Sir James Frazer's *The Golden Bough*, on "The Soul as a Mannikin," and "The Soul as Shadow and Reflection."

"What shall a man give in exchange for his soul?"

"What shall it profit a man, if he gain the whole world and lose his own soul?

"Of all the things a man has, next to the Gods," said Plato in *The Laws*, "his soul is the most divine and most truly his own . . . which no one honors as he should."

"Let parents, then," he said, "bequeath to their children not riches, but the spirit of reverence."

That curious book, *The Golden Bough*, justly famous for its monumental and skillful ordering of materials, seems from a later perspective to be somewhat coldly rigid and dogmatic in its reasoning and somewhat less than sympathetic toward the past, which it views impassively from an Olympian height of nineteenth-century enlightenment. In it all savages are crude, all magic is black magic, all religion is bloody. Frazer finds the tapestry of history woven of three colors, he finally tells us in *Farewell to Nemi*: black, red, and white—black for magic, red for religion, and white, the pure white light of truth, for science. The golden bough, toward the identity of which Frazer leads the reader relentlessly through hundreds of pages, turns out finally to be a parasitic mistletoe on a sacred oak mistakenly worshiped as a god.

Sir James thought there was a prereligious stage in man's development, when he was more akin to the modern scientist. So he writes, at the beginning of the fourth chapter, "Wherever sympathetic magic occurs in its pure unadulterated form, it assumes that in nature one event follows another necessarily and invariably without the intervention of any spiritual or personal agency. Thus its fundamental conception is identical with that of modern science."

The fundamental conception of modern science, to Frazer, was that "the course of nature is determined by the operation of immutable laws acting mechanically."

This may have been at that time the working hypothesis of the physical sciences, but was hardly a final word about man and the universe.

One wonders whether "immutable laws acting mechanically" could account for a Shakespeare, or even for the humblest and forever blessed anonymous originator of a nursery rhyme?

Yet the reading of *The Golden Bough*—the white spaces between as well as the rows of print—is a rich and enriching experience. In its great succession of poetic myths and seasonal ceremonies, we trace a lineage of gods who bring sustenance of corn and wine to those whose lives are dependent upon forces beyond their own brief volition. We trace the long and ancient lineage of Christ as the sacrificial lamb. We go joyfully with the shepherds to Bethlehem, the House of Bread. With the women we climb the hill of skulls to the Man of Sorrows on the cross. With the disciples gathered together in Jerusalem at Eastertide we rejoice in the resurrection.

One becomes deeply involved, in *The Golden Bough,* in the poetry of seasonal ceremonials, whose cycle is akin to the path of the mystic. Everything done ritually or believed mythically was metaphor and symbol, the bread and wine of real relationship and inner need.

We speak, in philosophical and theological language, of God as the ground of being

—a metaphorical expression derived from our relation to and dependence upon the earth, the very ground beneath our feet.

The mystic speaks of spiritual aridity—likened to lack of rain, dryness, and sterility, parched plant life, seed unquickened in the ground. In T. S. Eliot's *The Waste Land,* a religious poem, the spiritual aridity of our times is likened to a prolonged drought, mountains of rock without water, voices singing out of empty cisterns and exhausted wells. It is thunder and lightning that bring the promise of possible new life to come.

The traditional church calendar of feast days follows a seasonal pattern as old as man and man's religions. In the spring with its resurrection of plant life, in the summer with its growth under a hot sun and its need for rain ("Every prayer is a prayer for rain, for if it does not rain, the people perish"), in the autumn with its harvesting and storing for winter, in snow-time with its long underground sleep and provisions dwindling, man's relation to the earth and sky, to all invisible powers, was a direct daily preoccupation such as modern urban man can hardly imagine.

The beautiful old superstitions of a former age may be irrecoverable as a poetry believed in. Yet there is a pagan in every one of us, waiting to be allowed to make his gesture and to say his word. And we may also, when the eyes of our eyes are opened, with William Blake see a world in a grain of sand, and with Pierre Teilhard de Chardin see in "inanimate" matter no mere "it," but the inexhaustible potential of everything that is, charged with creative power. "Over everything which is to grow, to flower, to ripen this day, say again the words, *This is my body.*"

The Tao men describe
Is not the eternal Tao.
The names men give
Cannot designate the Nameless.

The myriads of named things
Spring from an inexhaustible matrix.
These point beyond themselves
To the all-encompassing Unity.

Of Nature, the Mystic Mother,
And the unknown, nameless Original,
Men may speak as though they were separate;
But these distinctions vanish into the abyss.

The enigma of things deepens
Into the Fathomless beyond.
From mystery to mystery is the gateway
Into the streaming wonder of existence.[4]

10. Everything Waits to be a Sacrament

Men may see or feel in all things something more than the things themselves. So the sacramental comes into existence.

A sacrament, our chatechism said, is "an outward and visible sign of an inward and spiritual grace." The outward and visible attributes, which can never be the whole of existence or the whole of experience, are balanced and completed by attributes "inward and spiritual." Between them is the connecting link of a sign, something seen, touched, handled, eaten, painted, sung, danced, or spoken. The sign, like the arrow on the weather vane, points to something beyond itself and invisible.

The earliest and most universal of sacraments, far-off precursor of the Christian Communion or Eucharist, was the sacrament of eating. Early man was vividly aware of the fact that other life makes our food. Eating, he partook of other life and was strengthened by it. Eating, he gathered with others around a common board and thus

89

partook also of the invisible bread of mutuality. In partaking, each a morsel, of the sacred totem animal, men experienced the mystery of a strength beyond theirs becoming their own. The primitive tribesman, we are told, identified himself with the totem animal, which he did not kill and eat except ceremonially and at stated intervals, in order to have a mediator and intercessor for him with the animal kingdom. Men, in order to be men, had to hedge with restraints the shedding of blood and eating of meat. Even when they killed necessarily in order to live, they sought forgiveness. They consecrated or debrutalized the natural process, as Professor R. R. Marett puts it, by representing it as a moral relation, a giving and receiving of help in times of need.[1] In the sacrament of eating men could express their desire to be at one with the invisible powers to which they looked for their daily bread. So men strove to overcome the brutalizing effects of violence. So they sought to have communion with each other and with other forms of life.

Other sacraments of primitive folk had to do with fighting, mating, educating, ruling, covenanting, healing, dying. The sacrament, says Dr. Marett, is the most dynamic of all ritual forms, having to do with the consecrating of natural functions to the ends of a better life together, thus bringing into play the latent moral energy of the persons and the community.

The Catholic Church has seven sacraments, all of ancient lineage: Baptism, bringing a child into the covenanted community; Confirmation, introducing the child to a personally responsible role, as in the immemorial puberty rites; Marriage, bringing a mated couple likewise into a responsible relation to society; the Eucharist or Mass, the immemorial sacrament of eating, with the divine grace of communion and thanksgiving; Penance, for forgiveness and restoration of relationship; Extreme Unction, the rite of passage to the beyond; Holy Orders, or investiture into the priesthood. In the Eastern Church these are called mysteries.

The danger of sacramentalism was that the rituals could pass from relation to life into becoming something in and of and for themselves, independent of the life-situations from which they grew. This is what Martin Buber meant when he said that "the principal danger of man is 'religion' "—that is, making it a day apart, a thing apart, a place apart, pushing the sacred off into a corner as something no longer related to one's lived, everyday life and its consecration.[2]

Rituals so remote from a life-situation that their origin is forgotten tend to become a substitute, a form of vicarious action, instead of a hallowing and a celebrating of the lived life of the everyday. The forms that were meant to consecrate life to God, as Martin Buber put it, become the means of separating it from God. Martin Buber feared making forms and rituals and observances an "It," valued for themselves instead of celebrations and consecrations of the work, deeds, and relationships of real everyday life.

The extreme danger of Judaism, in its scattered and isolated European ghetto existence, was that it would live only in the past, to which it looked for every sacred antecedent; or only in the future, to which it looked with longing for a restoration of

Israel. In the seventeenth century crisis of hopelessness for the many followers of Sabbatai Zevi after his defection to Islam, came an east-European revival called Hasidism, from which at its best Martin Buber took the good cue of religion as a hallowing of the everyday, with the aim of sacramentalizing the whole of man's life.

The sacramental again became, beautifully and simply in many of the Hasidic communities, something very real: to eat in holiness, to savor the taste of one's bread in holiness, to enjoy one's marriage bed in holiness so that the Shekinah or radiance of God hovers over it, to study and to work in holiness, because of doing and sharing with love. So one does well, for the sake of doing well, with love and joy and praise in one's heart, like "Enoch the cobbler, who with each stitch of his bodkin as it sowed the upper leather and the sole together, joined together God and His Shekinah."

If there is a way to renewal in religion, it is in the sacramental spirit, a sense of the sacramental possibility in everything as an outward and visible sign of an inward and spiritual grace.

"There is less difference than people suppose between research and adoration." The scientist in his laboratory, seeking the truth of a thing, could feel himself to be performing a sacramental act.

In the *New York Times* of March 18, 1965 was reported the charming story of a "happening" during a discussion of scientists, philosophers, educators, artists, and laymen under the auspices of the Foundation for Integrative Education, under the title, "Science and the Recovery of Meaning." During the final session of this six-evening series of discussions, "an elderly man," Dr. Arthur Moor, a retired editorial researcher, arose and captured the audience, said the *Times* reporter, by telling of a teacher who gathered a group of children around him "to start botany."

It was toward springtime, Dr. Moor said, and the teacher said, "I saw something the other day and I wonder if any of you have seen it? If you know it, don't say what it is. I went out and saw it coming up from the ground, about ten inches high, and on top of it was a little round ball of fluff, and if you went woof, a whole galaxy of stars flew out."

"Now what was it like before the little ball of stars appeared?"

One said it was a little yellow flower, like a sunflower, only very small.

"And what was it like before that?"

A little girl said it was like a tiny green umbrella, half closed, with a yellow lining showing.

"Yes, but what was it like before that?"

One of them said it was a little rosette of green leaves coming out of the ground.

"Now, do you all know what it is?"

They roared back, "Dandelion!"

"And did you ever pick dandelions?"

Most of them said yes, but the teacher said, "No, you can't pick a dandelion. That's impossible. A dandelion is all these things you mentioned, and more, so whatever you picked, you got only a fragment of something or other. You can't pick a dandelion, because a dandelion isn't a thing; it's a performance. And you know, every living thing is a performance—even you."

Such a story, delightful to children of any age, could open our eyes to what puzzled many in Martin Buber's *I and Thou*, when he said that the I-Thou relation could happen not only between persons, but also between a person and other living things, or even an inanimate object, which at the moment is more than an object. "Inanimate things" are a performance too, as are all living things—a performance, in the ultimate sense, of the one ground of being in all.

So a scientist, seeking to recognize truly the performance of a thing, may be engaged in a sacramental act, only awaiting the recognition and the participation of others.

Or the artist, seeking in line, color, music, dance, sculpture, or verse to express his intuitions of dandelions that cannot be picked, may be performing a sacramental act, only awaiting our participation in it.

The fundamental sacrament, according to Martin Buber, is mutual confirmation: "To pass from person to person the heavenly bread of self-being."

"Everything waits to be a sacrament." It is because a dandelion cannot be picked, because something more dwells in everything than we can grasp or name or handle, that the world and everything in it may become a sacrament, a host, indicating a presence.

> But look how beautiful—
> Look how beautiful are all the things

that He does. His signature
Is the beauty of things.[3]

In the sacrament of praise a human being responds to the light, as a flower opens to the sun.

A most striking commentary on "It is a good thing to sing praises" in the Ninety-second Psalm, is a little poem by Rainer Maria Rilke, which reads in translation:

O tell us, poet, what do you do?—I praise.
But those dark, deadly, devastating ways,
how do you bear them, suffer them?—I praise.
And then the Nameless, beyond guess or gaze,
how do you call it, conjure it?—I praise.
And whence your right, in every kind of maze,
in every mask, to remain true?—I praise.
And that the mildest and the wildest ways
know you like star and storm?—Because, I praise.[4]

In the Hebrew *Kaddish* the sacrament of praise is brought into the house of mourning.

In exile, in the trenches, out of the depths of personal sorrow or affliction, man can still lift up his spirit in admiration.

One of the most remarkable expressions of this in all literature is in the opening passage of Second Isaiah.

A despairing voice says:
  "What shall I cry?
All flesh is grass,
And the goodliness thereof as the flower of the fields:
    The grass withereth,
    The flower fadeth,
    Because the breath of the Lord bloweth upon it:
Surely the people is grass!

And then a second voice replies:
  "The grass withereth,
    The flower fadeth:
But the word of our God shall stand for ever."[5]

A similar breathtaking transition occurs in the 103d Psalm. The creature who knows he is akin to the lowliest and most transient, the grass that withers and the flower that fades, lifts up his heart in adoration to the transcendent and the everlasting. This is the selfless, sublime act of the absurdly, incurably religious man, for which he receives nothing and yet has all.

11. A Secular Megalopolis?

Messianic expectations sometimes cater to a natural human weakness of procrastination, of compensatory dreams about the future. Things will get worse before they become better. Or things inevitably must get worse, as Calvinists, Fundamentalists, and Marxists would say. The old war between devils and angels becomes, in Marxism, a class war. Zoroastrian dualism is turned into a stark alternative between exploited and exploiter, worker and capitalist. Armageddon is the coming revolution. The millennium, after the great purge, will be the classless society of the future, where justice is so perfectly achieved that the state withers away as no longer of any use. This pattern is to repeat itself until the whole world becomes a Communist Zion.

An exaggerated Christian fear of communism as the inevitable wave of the future, "the anti-Christ," could well be due, especially among the Fundamentalists, to a deeply implanted and persistent idea of inevitable progression toward Armageddon.

The clay that clings to the messianic ideal may be seen, even in its most exalted scriptural expressions, as a human—all-too-human—looking forward to a time when the tables will be turned, a "getting even" in a sudden overturn from the bottom to the top, from the defeated to the victorious. So in the great Song of Zion Redeemed of Second Isaiah:

> Strangers shall build up thy walls,
>   And their kings shall serve thee. . . .
> And the sons of them that afflicted thee
>   Shall come bending unto thee;
> All they that despised thee
>   Shall bow themselves down at the soles of thy feet.[1]

The fainthearted among the early Christians, in a time of dire persecution, were supposed to be strengthened and encouraged by the vision in the Apocalypse of St. John of Patmos, wherein Rome, the great harlot drunk with the blood of martyrs and seated on a scarlet animal with seven heads and seven horns, is cast into a lake of fire and brimstone.

Communism, a "corporate self-worship" or a "quasi religion," along with humanism of the delimiting rational and positivistic type, would build for man only a well-ordered secular city. Perhaps the most absurdly naïve of all expectations is that an "atheistic Christianity" will redeem the secular metropolis, under the inspiration and the stimulus of that great secular literature, the Bible. What seems more likely to be in the offing is megalopolis, with pockets of vice, poverty, disease, and discontent, where people are estranged from nature and from each other, sterile and suppressed as to their vitality and their emotions, intellectually arid and uncreative, morally arrogant and hard.

Since Nietzsche, in *Thus Spake Zarathustra*, broke the news to his readers that God is dead, this obituary notice, considered premature in its day, has made recent headlines. It was over the Christian God that Nietzsche sprinkled ashes and pronounced a committal service near the end of the nineteenth century, and now, along with the Marxists, a host of influential writers and thinkers, existentialist and humanist—together with not a few theologians and teachers of religion in colleges and divinity schools—have joined the funeral procession.

This, when one stops to think about it, is neither strange nor new. The doubts of the humanists and the existentialists, of post-Christian or postmodern or "the fourth" man, have agitated the minds of many through all the centuries of human history, and are vigorously expressed in the biblical book called Ecclesiastes, in some of the Psalms, in the drama of Job. Such doubts often led to pessimism and fatalism. "All is vanity and chasing after wind," has been reechoed a thousand thousand times, sometimes by thoughtful, sensitive, and profoundly unhappy persons whose nerve ends were painfully exposed to the misery and injustice they saw all around them. Of Thomas Hardy it was said that it was the acute sensitiveness of his charity that made him a skeptic. He could not believe in a good God who not only would allow such cruelties to exist, but who, if all-powerful, must be considered their ultimate source. "The President of the Immortals had had his sport with Tess," was savagely directed against such a presumed personal cosmic dictator. With Hardy, in calmer moments, it was: "Not to care is not to know."

Whether the victims of idol-smashers or of their own doubts, whether lost to their gods by exile or by having outgrown them, men have often been lost and lonely and shivering under cold and indifferent stars.

Modern men, in Darwinism and in astronomy's revelation of the stunningly unimaginable dimensions of the known universe, have had onslaughts of this kind that to many exposed and sensitive persons were overwhelming. There are vivid expressions of this experience in modern writing.

In Wilbur Daniel Steele's story, *The Man Who Saw Through Heaven,* a missionary about to depart for Africa is subjected to the spiritual earthquake of an evening in an astronomical observatory, where he is shattered by the concept of differing orders of magnitude, a universe in an atom, and what he had thought of as heaven receding at the speed of light into a fathomless universe. A search party several years later in British East Africa follows his trail from one tribal village to another by way of curious mud sculptures he has left behind him—"models of the universe." These, evolving from protoplasmic blobs to monstrous lizards, turtles, and crocodiles, begin more and more to take on something of the human shape, until finally in the village where he died, "our

Father Witch," as the natives there call him, has left a final sculpture: his last overlord of cosmic categories, fashioned in his own image. It is man-sized, seated on a bench or throne of mud. One finger of one hand had been done with much care. It wears an opal, set in a silver ring. This hand is lifted, and over it the head is bent.

"The figure was crudeness itself, but in the relation between the bent head and the lifted finger there was a sense of scrutiny one would have said no genius of mud could ever have conveyed. An attitude of interest centered in that bauble, intense and static, breathless and eternal all in one—penetrating to its bottom atom, to the last electron, to a hill upon it, and to a two-legged mite about to die. Marking (yes, I'll swear to the incredible) the sparrow's fall."[2]

After this last sculpture the shattered missionary had been able to pray again, "Our Father which art in heaven."

So he had come to the "comforting illusion within the warm glow of which the more tender-minded intellectuals seek to shelter themselves from the icy winds of the universe."

Stephen Crane's remarkable story entitled *The Open Boat*, where, after a shipwreck, a captain, a cook, an oiler, and a correspondent are tossed about in a little boat by mountainous waves, is a parable of the effect upon many persons in our time of a universe suddenly grown too vast, too terrifyingly indifferent to be a home for man's spirit.

In this tale four casually acquainted human beings, thrown together by catastrophe and surrounded by towering menace, experience now a poignancy of comradeship they had never known before. Against the cosmic chill men draw closer together to keep warm. So they huddled in bomb shelters during the war. "You see, we have only each other. If there is no help outside, all the more need to help one another. If from the indifferent stars there comes no answering voice, let us address ourselves to our fellow men." This is a good humanist happening. Even the pious Hasidist, however, knew this "value of atheism," as when he taught: "If someone comes to you asking for help, do not say, 'Trust in God; He will help you,' but act as if there were no God and none but you to lend a hand."

Another good humanist happening is to see, over against this inscrutable and indifferent universe, human courage and nobility all the grander for its stark isolation.

> For Mercy has a human heart;
>   Pity, a human face;
> And Love, the human form divine;
>   And Peace, the human dress.

So wrote William Blake in *Songs of Innocence*, and humanists have taken this poem, "The Divine Image," for one of their hymns—with reason enough, for such attributes as love, mercy, justice, and goodness were first discovered in human experience and then ascribed to deity.

But William Blake went on to write another divine-image poem, in *Songs of Experience*:

> Cruelty has a human heart,
>   And Jealousy a human face;
> Terror the human form divine,
>   And secrecy the human dress.
>
> The human dress is forged iron,
>   The human form a fiery forge,
> The human face a furnace sealed,
>   The human heart its hungry gorge.

The dilemma of the humanist, as he stands at Dachau before the crematories, is to have to say in his heart: "This was done by members of the human race, and therefore what the Nazis did I did too, or was capable of doing." The true believer of our time is the one who, much as he wished not to, looked into the abyss of the concentration camps and the gas chambers, into the abyss of My Lai, and saw there himself, the human image. He is a humbler and also a safer person than the one who turns away or shuts his eyes.

Storm Jameson, in the preface to Ann Frank's diary, says that mankind's greatest cruelties have been in the service of an idea. "Men learned early," she says, "to press a doctrine over ears and eyes, so that they could torture without being distracted by the victim's agony."

> Your church was the first to show
> that you can burn men just like coke.

When Iceland was first visited by King Olaf and a bishop, Iceland's leaders were taken prisoner and offered Christian baptism. When they refused, a hot iron in the mouth and a pan of glowing coals on the stomach were used as persuaders.

Fontana, in Rolf Hochhuth's *The Deputy and the Jews,* who blames the church for being the first incinerator says, "If I knew that He looks on . . . I would hate Him." Man's cruelties are an embarrassment to his humanism, a stumbling block to his theodicies.

Perhaps *isms*, indicating doctrines about, or doctrines in a sort of final way, are today of all things most dispensable. Theism, after all, means an "ism" about God, and humanism an "ism" about man. Both have suffered in our century.

We are born into a generation that requires us to look into two abysses.

The one is the abyss of ourselves. It is deeper than we had supposed. The depths to which the human being can sink have opened up in recent times to our unwilling gaze. Paul Tillich pionts out that there is something hopeful also about such demonic depth in the human: it does away with easy optimism; it means that we are not simple creatures whose possibilities are soon or easily exhausted. There are corresponding possible heights. St. Augustine was right; but so also was Pelagius, as the Church tacitly acknowledged in taking up instruction. The London anthropologist R. R. Marett finds "Faith, Hope and Charity in Primitive Religion" in his book of that title, but has to balance his account with chapters on fear, lust, and cruelty.

The other abyss we must look into is the abyss of infinite being, in which all the gods are swallowed up. This is a good, a necessary, a humbling experience, as it was to the forest sages of India in the century of the Upanishads.

The people who refuse to look into these two abysses are not safe for our time. Unbelievers, those who cling to some "ism," are dangerous in this nuclear age.

The need is for those true believers who doubt much and cannot accept an easy good or an easy God. They see themselves in perspective. They are not a humanity turned in upon itself, but aware of kinship with other creatures and able to respond to the transhuman magnificence of things.

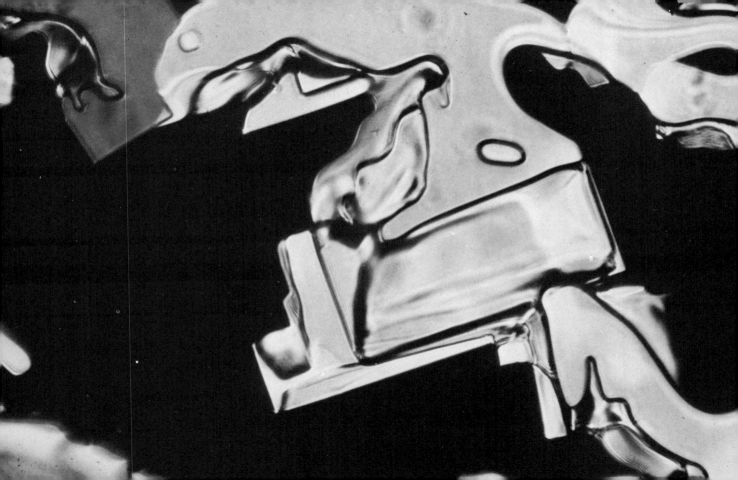

12. Tao Te Ching and Counterculture

Confucianism and Taoism have been called the two wings of Chinese thought. They may also be called two ways of reacting to a time of troubles. Both Confucius and Lao Tzu taught in periods of disintegration, of rival war lords and warring feudal states.

Confucius anxiously tried to set things right, and gave China so much by way of practical wisdom that he was given the title, long after he died, of the First Holy One. His teaching may be succinctly summed up in "Mutual consideration is the basis of society," and "At the root of all else is the person."

Lao Tzu taught by withdrawal, saying in effect, "What shall it profit a man to struggle against this disorder, and thereby lose his own soul?"

Among the ancient Chinese, as early perhaps as a thousand years before the Christian era, philosophers distinguished between an active and a passive principle in all things, *yang* and *yin*. Of these two interacting energy modes, *yang* was masculine and *yin* feminine. Confucius' reaction to a troubled time might be called the *yang* reaction: a masculine attempt to front the storm though it break one in two. Lao Tzu's reaction could be called the *yin* reaction: being "wife" to the storm, bending with it so as not to break, yielding to it until its force is spent.

"What shall a man give in exchange for his soul?" Lao Tzu's response to a time of trouble was that of exploring the potential and the meaning of one's own personal existence to the full. "I went to the woods," said Thoreau, "because I wished to live deliberately, to front only the essential facts of life, and see if I could not learn what it had to teach, and not, when I came to die, discover that I had not lived." Lao Tzu likewise became a recluse for a purpose. He was thereby saying to the world, "The life you are nurturing is also the life you are destroying. It is a frustrated, imprisoned life, whether held down by oppression or smothered in luxury."

Chuang Tzu, the great Taoist who wrote in the second century after the death of his master, gives a witty, biased, and charming account of a meeting between Confucius and Lao Tzu, wherein the latter likens Chinese civilization to an artificial pond drying up and leaving the fish stranded. On returning from this visit, Confucius, so the story goes, did not speak for three days. Then, when questioned by a disciple as to how he had admonished Lao Tzu, he replied, "I saw a dragon." Birds that fly may be overtaken by an arrow; fish that swim may be caught in a net; the swift hare may be snared in a noose; but who can take the dragon as, bestriding wind and clouds, he rises toward heaven?[1]

Confucius, who was not all housekeeper and activist but one of the wisest of men, would doubtless have been attracted and impressed had he met Lao Tzu, which hardly seems possible.

The Taoist in Confucius once asked four of his disciples what they would like to do, if some ruler would give them the opportunity. The first answered that he would like to straighten out, within three years, a large state having ten thousand chariots which was being invaded and suffering famine. The second, more modestly, would like to administer a small country to which, also within three years, he would bring peace and prosperity. The third, still more modestly, would like to assist with the ceremonials of state, along with the princes of the sovereign. The fourth disciple, who had meanwhile been fingering his lute, was asked, "Tien, what are your wishes?"

Tien replied, "In this the last month of spring I would like to go with the children to bathe in the river *I*, enjoy the breeze along the rain altars, and then return home with them singing."

The Master heaved a sigh and said, (according to the account), "You are a man after my own heart!"[2]

Confucius too could long for simplicity and on a beautiful spring day desire nothing so much as to immerse himself with children in real waters, share their joy in a pilgrimage to the rain altars, and return home singing.

Lao Tzu and many of his early followers in China were dropouts, like many of our youth today. The times were out of joint and could not be set straight—or if they could be forcibly bent into a better shape, it was hardly worth the effort. So they withdrew, in a time when retiring to one's own cottage and vegetable garden was somewhat easier than now. Said Lao Tzu, or one of his followers, in the Tao Teh Ching:

> No need to leave one's doorstep
>   To see the whole world.
> No need to run to the window
>   To observe Heaven's ways.
>
> The more one rushes about
>   The less one sees and knows.
> The further one travels
>   The more one flees the Center.
>
> The Sage has arrived
>   Without ever having departed.
> He perceives without roving;
>   He puts being before doing.[3]

There is a wonderful relaxed quietness in the Tao Te Ching, which begins to steal into one's soul as one reads and ponders. To withdraw, to drop out, to live in a secluded cottage or a monastery for a time, should be one of the rhythms of our lives. We in the West tend to be activists, to strain after results, to hurry toward completion, to rush to publication, to exploit talents prematurely, to stimulate artificially the birth pangs of creation. We are like the man to whom Chuang Tzu said, "You expect to hear an egg crow at daybreak."

Some of us in the West are only now beginning to learn "the usefulness of uselessness." The Shang Mountain tree, of which Chuang Tzu tells us that its leaf was bitter, its branches too crooked for rafters, its trunk of such irregular grain as to be valueless for coffins, was a tree good for nothing, and so it endured. "A wise man will follow its example."

There is the story also of the man who fished, not for fish, but for fun. This struck Wen Wang, on a provincial tour of inspection, as a most unusual display of wisdom. (The Chinese honored these recluses, although seldom following their example, much as Americans have honored Thoreau.) Somehow Wen Wang persuaded the old fisherman to take over the administration of the province. The old man altered none of the existing statutes. He issued no unjust regulations. He followed the Taoist philosophy of laissez-faire, "let things alone," and after three years, when Wen Wang returned, all was in order.

Wen Wang then asked the old man, "Can such government be extended over the empire?"

The old man, so the story goes, made no reply. He then abruptly took leave, and by the evening of the same day had disappeared, never to be heard of again.

He was wise, after all. Like Lao Tzu, who disappeared over the western horizon riding a blue water buffalo.

One can readily see why the Tao Te Ching has had a very special appeal to dropouts, young or old, or to the makers of a new subculture who refuse to throw their lives into the rat race. As Chuang Tzu said it long ago: "Don't be a man enslaved by men for the sake of his cleverness, like a dog good at catching foxes, whom they run to death."

This was not frivolous advice. Life is precious, and the worth of a thing, as Thoreau said, ought to be reckoned in terms of how much life it costs.

"If a man nowadays," said Chuang Tzu "were to load a crossbow with a priceless pearl in order to shoot a bird a thousand *yin* away, everybody would ridicule him. And why? Because he would be using something of immense value to acquire something comparatively worthless. Well, then, isn't life of infinitely greater value than a pearl?"

Who is the escapist—the man who is so busy, so perpetually on the go that he is likened by Chuang Tzu to one who is afraid of his own shadow and drops dead vainly trying to outrun it, or the hidden sage of the Tao Te Ching, who under his coarse cloth carries precious jade?

The Tao Te Ching, says Lin Yutang, teaches "the wisdom of appearing foolish, the success of seeming to fail, the strength of weakness, the advantage of lying low, the futility of contending for power."[4] This book, he says further, contains the oldest expression in the world of the idea or the art of camouflage—that is, of putting on protective coloring and seeming to be other than you are. This seems to have meant, in the Tao Te Ching, to give the appearance of being utterly unimportant: then nobody will bother to push you around. Or, it's better to look less important than you are than to be less important than you look. Or, better still, it's important to live, and put on whatever togs will interfere least with that. (What we need, said Thoreau, is not new clothes, but new wearers of clothes.)

Taoism is older than Lao Tzu, as Confucianism is older than Confucius. In the classics we come upon the spirit of both in the doctrine of *wu-wei*, or "let things alone." This meant, in part: Let the individual follow his own bent; let the local community develop its own resources; let the province govern itself without interference from above. So the Chinese were able to hold together a great empire through several thousand years, with incomparably less coercion than any other large empire of the past. An ancient maxim, older than Confucianism and Taoism and known to both, is cited in the Tao Te Ching: "Govern an empire as you would fry a small fish." That is, let it alone, don't fuss over it and keep turning it, or you will reduce it to paste.

Lao Tzu extended the doctrine of *wu-wei* also to the personal life. Don't fuss over yourself too much. Let things happen in you, rather than try to make them happen. Be quiet. Be patient. Don't press. Wait for the water to clear. Give your talents time to mature.

The Tao Te Ching has been called the Sermon on the Mount of China. In form, in flavor, in philosophy, it differs from, more than it resembles, the Sermon on the Mount of St. Matthew. Yet there are interesting parallels.

The spirit of "be not anxious for the morrow" and "consider the lilies" is here.

As Jesus taught humility, meekness, poverty of spirit, so Lao Tzu taught the importance of being an empty vessel, waiting to be filled.

> Humble yourself, and remain whole.
> Be willing to bend, and remain unbroken.
> Empty yourself, and find fulfilment.[5]

As Jesus taught that the last shall be first, the humble shall be exalted, and the greatest shall be servant of all, so Lao Tzu taught that the sage is humble and serviceable, like a brook.

> He seeks the lower levels.
> He is a valley to which things flow.[6]

Both taught the virtue of noncontention and noncompetitiveness, the overcoming of hatred with love, of evil with good.

The New Testament paradox of the strength of the weak and the weakness of the strong is here:

> Nothing under heaven is softer
> And more yielding than water.
> Yet when it attacks things hard and resistant,
> There is not one of them that can withstand.

> So the strong are overcome by the weak,
> The hard by the yielding,
> The haughty by the humble.[7]

Both teach the way of nonviolence. Eight of the short chapters or meditations in the Tao Te Ching are devoted specifically to this theme. The tenor of the whole is that the Tao of heaven and the Tao or true way for man is the way of nonviolence, noncontention.

> An army's harvest is thorns and brambles.[8]

> When Tao is abandoned,
> War horses are bred on the common.[9]

> To exult in victory
> Is to delight in slaughter.
> Let the war dead be mourned
> Of friend and foe alike.
> Let a victory be celebrated
> With the funeral rite.[10]

> Better to be invaded than to invade.
> Where two equally matched armies meet,
> The one that yields wins.[11]

The most remarkable of these meditations on nonviolence holds a unique place in the scriptures of mankind, and should be taught in all academies to all budding statesmen and diplomats. It reads:

> If a great kingdom humble itself
> Before a smaller kingdom,
> The latter becomes its willing prize.
>
> If a small kingdom humble itself
> Before a greater kingdom,
> The greater is won over.
>
> The one, in order to gain, humbles itself.
> The other, already small, becomes greater.
>
> Should the larger kingdom desire only
> That men be brought together and nourished,
> The smaller kingdom will enter willingly
> Into the common service.
>
> If both are to serve the one desire,
> The great must learn humility.[12]

Strangely enough, of the eighty-one meditations in the Tao Te Ching, eleven, or nearly a seventh, have to do with government—an astonishing number for an anthology by quietistic followers of a legendary Sage who ended a brief career in governmental service by withdrawing to the western mountains. But Lao Tzu and his inner circle were profoundly concerned that the state should not be all. His ideal was "lazy government." Unlike Confucius, who sought his answer through vigorously virtuous government, Lao Tzu wanted as little government, as little interference with the life of the people, as possible.

Yet the antithesis is not so sharp as the historic controversy between rival schools would have us suppose. Confucius, after all, taught that *shu*, mutual consideration, never doing to others what one would not have done to oneself, is the basis of the good society. "Among the means for the regeneration of mankind, said Confucius, "those with noise and show are of the least effect." He wanted government by self-government, by the force of good example, rather than by coercion and intervention. "From the Son of Heaven down to the people, at the root of all else is the cultivation of the person."

Lao Tzu also put the cultivation of the person at the root of all else. But the methods and the philosophies diverge. Confucius sought that cultivation in imitating the illustrious ancestors, in holding up before men the model of an idealized golden age in the past. He was a transmitter, as he said, who wished to build culture through a stabilizing tradition. This had its great value; and his way prevailed, in a more extreme fashion than he had envisaged, through the filial piety which was the cement of the longest-lived civilization we have yet seen.

Lao Tzu, on the other hand, sought the cultivation of the person in the spontaneities of love, intuition, mystical realization, guided by a Tao or Way which is not traditional but natural and discoverable within. The term *Tao* is used for a trinity: the Nameless and Fathomless Original, its manifestation as "the Way and its Power" in nature, its presence and discovery within the person.

Men relate themselves to the Cosmic Mystery beyond all imagining or conceptualization through nature or the Mystic Mother, known through her sons and the myriad things of this world. Men must live "according to nature." When they do not do so, they are like swimmers struggling against a strong current.

The ruler who rules according to Tao will say little and accomplish much, doing things effortlessly, like nature, and keeping himself out of the picture, like the sage.

> The good ruler rules so inconspicuously
> That, although his influence is everywhere,
> The people are hardly aware of its source.
>
> The weak ruler wishes to be flattered.
> The bad ruler wishes to be feared.
> Where the ruler distrusts the people
> The people in turn will distrust him,
> Who then demands their loyalty.

> The good ruler talks little,
> And when his work is done,
> His aims accomplished,
> People will say:
> "Look! Things were so of themselves."
> Or, "Look! We did this."[13]

The sage, who also talks little and teaches by what he is, is rich in inner resources. The Mystic Mother, gateway to the Cosmic Mystery beyond, with gateways also to the mystery within, is "the ever-renewing source upon which men may draw, and the more they take, the more remains." Hence, "the inward mysterious power of those who live from the center."

By "closing the door" and "stopping the apertures," by "entering into the Quiet within," by "using the light to return to the Light," by "embracing the One," one comes to the ineffable experience of Tao.

The Taoist utopia pictured near the end of this brief, cryptic scripture is realizable, one may say, only in small, withdrawn subculture communities.

> Let it be a small country with unpretentious houses.
> The few who dwell there govern themselves.
> They keep their records by knots in a cord,

And enjoy their morning and evening chores.
They make their own simple clothing.
Their home-baked bread tastes good to them.

Labor saving devices are discarded as useless.
Weapons of war may still be lying about,
But nobody bothers to pick them up.
Although they still have a few boats and carriages,
Nobody wants to go away in them.
The people are contented at home,
Why should they gad about?

The next town is so near
They can hear its dogs bark and roosters crow.
Yet the people grow old and die
Without ever bothering to go there.[14]

Such a utopia, rather questionable in its withdrawnness and provincialism, could exist only of course in the mind of the recluse who dreams it. Yet it is something very much more than the wistful daydream of a mystical anarchical sage. For if simplicity, attachment to the soil, intimate community, contentedness, the values of solitude and unregimented spontaneity, of self-realization, of seeing the whole world from one's doorstep, are to disappear from this earth, man will indeed have gained the whole world (in a totalitarian sense) but will have lost his own soul.

The Tao Te Ching is still a vividly contemporary warning against the idolatries of state, collective, institution (secular or sacred), and against a life wholly absorbed in affairs and merely horizontal in dimension.

Into our time it comes as an invitation, bidding us respect the Tao of nature, leading us to the inner and the living transcendence of realizing here and now, in this mortal and circumscribed existence of ours, a beyond the world that is yet within the world, and a beyond ourselves within ourselves:

> That with soundless music
> And a savor beyond taste or smell
> Has provisions that never fail.[15]

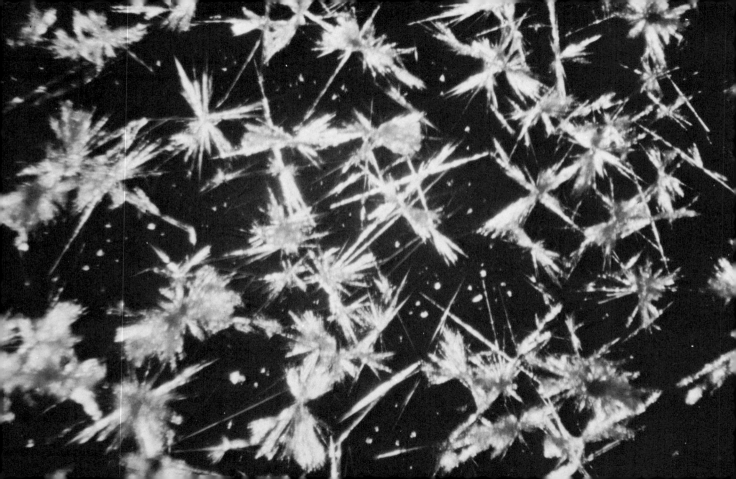

13. On the Sixth Day We Came

On the fifth day of creation, God said: "Let the waters bring forth abundantly the moving creature that hath life, and let fowl fly above the earth in the open firmament of heaven."[1]

The waters bringing forth, as the first great womb of life, take us to the Paleozoic Age of sea plants and fish, of the first amphibians, of land plants and reptiles.

There was a time, hundreds of millions of years ago, when an observer from another planet equipped with the most powerful of microscopes would have found no trace of mobile particles in the layer of water that covered the surface of this earth. But had he returned later in a somewhat cooler age, he would have found those same waters writhing with minute creatures, teeming with microscopic forms of life.

The fifth great day of God, in the animal kingdom before man, was timeless. There was no looking back to remembered days, no looking forward to days yet to come.

Adam had not yet made a world by naming it. This was the world of the biosphere, of proliferating protoplasm, of mysterious living units that divided to multiply.

Consciousness began late in that fifth day of creation, but it was a rudimentary, not a time-counting or time-spanning consciousness. A great mental calm reigned throughout the world in this fifth great day of God.

Over the landscape, where myriads of deer, antelope, and zebras, elephants and mastodons, roamed across fertile steppes and beasts of prey stalked them, the shadows of wings passed, but no smoke signals arose.

But one day a wisp of smoke curled upward, and earth's troubles began, with the human being and the beginning of time.

On that first strange morning of time Adam began to name things, and a world came into being.

The timeless age of innocence, the calm profusion, the sense of brotherhood with all creatures, this is the dimly remembered Garden of Eden from which man was driven forth to be man.

Adam eats of the fruit of the tree and learns that he must die. He comes to know guilt, anxiety, fear, remembrance of things past and hope of things to come. Said Emerson: "It is very unhappy, but too late to be helped, the discovery we have made that we exist. That discovery is called the Fall of Man."[2]

"And the Lord God caused a deep sleep to fall upon Adam, and he slept; and he took one of his ribs, and closed up the flesh instead thereof. And the rib, which the Lord God had taken from the man, made he woman, and brought her unto the man."[3]

The Hebrew word for rib is feminine, and means "side." One side of Adam was male, the other female. The primordial hermaphrodite was split in two, to become man and woman. Something like this happens to every person at a certain time of life, when the sex urge awakens and becomes powerful, and the individual becomes one-sidedly male or female. Early romantic love may be said to be the yearning of these two halves to become one, but hardly knowing as yet what that yearning is and somewhat fearful of it.

The life-force, then, would use us as its instrument, and can so utterly overwhelm us that for the time being we are not a particular Adam or a particular Eve, but just this surging life-passion taking over and having its own way with us.

As nature had to strew hundreds of acorns to make a tree—the chances were so slim and the hazards so great—so nature made the sex impulse imperious in order to stack the odds in favor of survival, over against hunger, drought, flood, earthquake, pestilence, and beasts of prey.

It took man a long time to cope with these external enemies, and then only to a limited extent. And yet, although he came on the sixth great day of God and not the fifth, he still tends like any other animal to breed up to the limit of his supplies.

The human population explosion, which began to gather momentum in the nineteenth century, is now upon us, with almost nothing being done as yet to slow it up. The rate is astonishing. If a limited atomic war should kill one hundred million people, that number, at the rate the human population is now increasing, could be replaced within three years. World War I, with its twenty million dead in four years, could continue on indefinitely and not affect the picture numerically.

The fifth day of creation, nature's balance, her calm profusion and wonderfully rich variety, are endangered by a creature who ate of the fruit of the tree of knowledge, knew himself to be king (and priest and prophet, no less), and decided that the earth was his to possess, to exploit, to subjugate.

"The prophets prophesy falsely, and the priests bear rule by their means; and my people love to have it so."[4]

"And God blessed them, and God said unto them, Be fruitful, and multiply, and replenish the earth, and subdue it: and have dominion over the fish of the sea, and over the fowl of the air, and over every living thing that moveth upon the earth."[5]

This God who gave man a land grant of all the earth, along with everything under and above the surface, animate and inanimate, was made in man's own image.

"And yet they think that their houses shall continue forever, and that their dwelling-places shall endure from one generation to another; they call their lands after their own names."[6]

How they say, "Mine!" My life, my wife, my children, my land, my God! The mystery and the beauty of everything they call "mine" eludes them. Even the flower they "own" shuts itself against them.

On the sixth day we came, building a city of millions, and another city of millions, and another and another, with a network of highways through urban sprawl between, until it becomes one vast megalopolis for hundreds of miles. The creature who came on the sixth day and said to himself, "The earth is mine, and I will possess and subdue it," threatens the destruction of the fifth great day of God.

> Some say the world will end in fire,
> Some say in ice.

Either would be cleanly and beautifully destructive compared to an end by pollution or being crowded off the earth by sheer numbers.

"In those days shall men seek death, and shall find it not; and shall desire to die, and death shall flee from them."[7]

In the meantime a grand nuclear explosion, accidentally triggered, could bring temporary relief.

"Alas, alas, that great city Babylon, that mighty city! for in one hour is thy judgment come."[8]

Not the sixth day only, O man! but also the first great day of God, when darkness was upon the face of the deep, and the Spirit of God moved upon the face of the waters, and God said, "Let there be light," and there was light.

Not the sixth day only, but also the parting of the waters in the second; and the earth bringing forth in the third; and the sun and moon and stars of the fourth; and the waters bringing forth abundantly in the fifth.

Religious man is to accept and to honor all the days of God's creation.

The arrival of man, as Julian Huxley and Pierre Teilhard de Chardin would have it, means "evolution become conscious of itself." Man holds in his hand the tiller of the world—a thrilling thought to Teilhard de Chardin, with his absurd but sublime belief in the profound identity between the forces of civilization and those of evolution, leading not to disintegration and death, but to a new break-through and a rebirth outside Time and Space.[9] More modestly those of a lesser faith or expectation of the future might hope for men wise enough, self-controlled and reverent enough, not to break irreparably the great chain of life, but to keep the earth beautiful and share it with other creatures.

"And God saw everything that he had made, and, behold, it was very good. And the evening and the morning were the sixth day."[10]

14. The Son of Man Comes Listening

The unspoken word at the beginning of speech, of all true address, is "Listen."

The unspoken word at the end of any meaningful breaking of silence is "Listen."

When Moses came down from the mountain to the children of Israel, they were noisily shouting and dancing around the golden calf. The unspoken word "Listen," a necessary prelude and precondition of heard speech, a requisite of communication, could not be heard in that idolatrous din.

The first tablet of the Law speaks of worshiping one transcendent Being only. Also of not taking the Name in vain: that is, not trivializing or profaning the Word, the sacredness of communication between being and being. The first tablet speaks also of "keeping his sabbath"; that is, having spaces of quiet and rest in one's days, of timelessness in time, of listening to the Word.

The word "Listen," before and after the first tablet of the Law, means that the act of creation is speech. The language of creation speaks in every living thing, in every molecule and atom of existence. We are to listen to what is said.

A good scientist is a good listener, a good asker of questions. Pure research is an ultimate discipline in listening to the language of creation.

The Dutch scholar Kornelis H. Miskotte, in his book *When the Gods Are Silent* speaks —along with many others of our time—of the eclipse, the utter silence of the God who once spoke. We live in a time of "chilling cosmic silence." But the gods, down through the centuries, have been a noisy lot, great thunderers and talkers. They were but images, or at their best, manifestations; let their silence be the beautiful silence of nature, where

> The heavens declare the glory of God,
> And the firmament showeth his handiwork.
> Day unto day uttereth speech,
> And night unto night showeth knowledge.
> There is no speech, nor words; their voice is not heard;
> Yet their voice goeth out through all the earth,
> And their words to the end of the world.

The Cosmic Silence is pregnant with speech, if man will but learn to listen.

There are other ways of listening to the language of creation than the scientific.

> The wild gander leads his flock through
> the cool night,

> *Ya-honk*, he says, and sounds it down to
>   me like an invitation.
> The pert may suppose it meaningless, but
>   I listening close
> Find its purpose and place up there toward
>   the wintry sky.[1]

There is a listening to things in their setting, in their relatedness, in their voice and place as part of the beauty of the whole. "Resonance to the All," said Pierre Teilhard de Chardin, "is the keynote of pure poetry and pure religion." Such listening is akin to prayer. As Simone Weil said, "Attention is an acceptable form of prayer." To pay attention, to be receptive: so we may come at times to a sabbath of listening, when things are taken back from the world of dissipation into the world of wholeness.

The second tablet of the Law has to do with one's neighbor: the brotherly covenant. "It is like unto the first." Here too the first unspoken word, and the last, is "Listen." To listen is to take the otherness of the other person seriously.

In this we are all sinners, many times every day, who need to be forgiven not seven times but seventy times seven. We indulge in monologue, speaking our piece and waiting, deaf, until the other person stops, when we begin again. If it is language that makes us human, one half of language is to listen. Dialogue is of the very substance of good relations.

The Son of Man comes listening.

"In the beginning was the Word."

"While all things were in quiet silence, and the night was in the midst of her course, thine Almighty Word, O Lord, came down from Heaven, out of thy royal throne."[2]

The birth of the word from silence was such an extraordinary event that early man had a sense of awe about language. There was magic in it, a hidden creative power that made worlds.

It is difficult today to regain this sense of wonder and awe before the transcendent origin, the creative power and potential of speech.

We have seen speech prostituted on a vast scale, used as a seductive persuader to spend one's life for baubles. We have seen it become hard and metallic, and hurled as a weapon. We have seen the ambitious and the powerful hire a new kind of mercenary, skilled in turning words into weapons, or counters in a game. We have seen language divorced from truth and from communication. We have seen it lose contact with creative silence and become mere noise. Some have said, even, that the age of speech is over. Language is dead. We are in a new age of sounds and shadows!

Alas, then, for civilization, of which the true substance, said Martin Buber, is dialogue.[3] Where there is real exchange, real heard speech and listening, real communication, there civilization grows and spreads. The greater nation culturally absorbs and enriches the smaller one. Where the frontiers are fortified to keep the barbarians out, where walls and battlements take the place of speech, the hungry barbarians finally break through and flood in, to take and ravage what should have been increased through sharing.

In war men turn from speech to violence. A "cold war" is a breakdown of dialogue —essentially grim speechlessness, or using words as weapons in what is called propaganda. The only real, effective enemy of war, said Martin Buber, is true speech, real dialogue. A time to talk is a time to listen: this has to take place between persons, between like and unlike groups within nations, between men and the nations of men, if this little planet-ship of ours is to continue on its journey with living creatures on board. Instead of trying to make other people over in our image, we should learn to listen.

The Son of Man comes listening. "I have given them thy word."

We need to learn again to listen, in order to be able again to speak.

Speech needs to be reborn in us, out of the silence, like the holy child of creativity and the festival of joy.

Yeats' "rough beast," in his "The Second Coming," "its hour come round at last," that "slouches towards Bethlehem to be born," is the new barbarian, the dumb slave of a speechless, computerized war machine.

15. *Sum Ergo Credo*

Everything that lives is holy.

If the doors of perception were cleansed, everything would appear to man as it is, infinite.

Every rock is deluged with deity.

In this stone lying at the temple gate, reside all the Buddhas that were and all the Buddhas to come.

Matter is holy, the matrix of existence. Immerse yourself in that ocean, plunge into it where it is deepest, struggle in its currents. For it cradled you long ago in your preconscious existence, and it can lift you up to God.

Every atom in the universe dances to Shiva's sacred drum.

To live is to thirst, to thirst for being.

And he showed me a pure river of water of life, clear as crystal, proceeding out of the throne of God and of the Lamb.

Mahayana is the Christ-Buddha's great ship of compassion, across the sea of sorrows.

The God who dies for us is the God who is resurrected in us.

Give us this day our daily bread.

Take, eat: this is my body, broken for you.

The Abyss, the Wholly Other, the Ineffable, the terrifying transcendency, is hard to live with.

So men keep trying to interpose nearer objects of worship.

Man must worship, and to render worship bearable or comfortable, he manufactures idols.

The holy mountains of this world are littered with wrecked and discarded idols.

A great and enduring idol is the idol-state. It demands and receives living sacrifices.

"Ask not what your country can do for you, but what you can do for your country."

To sacrifice mind and body in production, or blood and soul in warfare, is to gain participation in the divinity of the state.

The perfection of psuedoreligion is the military (believe in the idol and do not think): commandments, evocations; its sacred symbol the flag, its altar the battlefield; words as weapons; imposed discipline and hierarchy; consecrated slaughter; the ritual death of the hero-victim.

Men idolize themselves also, as individuals, to protect themselves against the depths within themselves, against terror of Self.

Another idol is the self-erected Truth, the self-selected exclusive Name, from the throne of which one can look down on all the gods and religions of others and pronounce them false.

The Abyss, the Mystery, the Ineffable, is hard to bear.

In tame religions, remote from their origins, there is no fear and trembling.

Tame religions dare not move beyond their small clearing in the endless forest.

In dead religions the fear of God is dead.

"Have compassion on me," said Job, "for the hand of God has touched me."

Without sorrows none becomes a Buddha.

"In what do you differ from others?" said the people to the suffering old woman in Africa. "God sits on the back of every one of us, and we cannot shake him off!"

I pray to God that he may quit me of God, for unconditioned being is above God and all distinctions.

We should contrive not to need to pray to God, asking for his grace and divine goodness, but take it without asking.

When I pray for something, I do not pray; when I pray for nothing, I really pray.

Such prayer is already an inward stirring toward new life.

Divided, how can one pray? How can one pray when another myself would be listening? That is why one should pray only in unknown words. Render enigma to enigma. Lift what is mystery in yourself to what is mystery in itself. There is something in you that is equal to what surpasses you.

Meditation, like a cool lake, has room for all the unexpected birds.

In stillness the world is renewed.

Men in their profoundest realizations do not talk, but stand silent side by side.

Consider the lilies, how they grow. When growth takes place as naturally and uninhibitedly as in the flower, when we are natural without trying to be natural, contemplatively relaxed, then the beautiful spontaneities of life, the direct and whole encounters of being, may come to pass.

A man in search of his Buddhahood is a man riding his ox in search of his ox.

Love blindly goes forward where reason stops.

Love knocks and enters, while knowledge waits outside.

Little blind stirrings of love can pierce the cloud of unknowing.

Only love can touch the mystery of another being.

Love ye the stranger, for ye were strangers in Egypt.

The world will explode unless it learns to love.

There is less difference than people suppose between research and adoration.

Blessed is he who becomes the harp of thy praise.

It is a great thing if a man can bring it about that God sings within him.

Nothing is as near to me as God is. His presence is my being.

To remain virgin forever is never to bear fruit. Let your soul be wife to God.

People for whom God is dead are people, alas, for whom God is dead.

The most precious thing is you in others and others in you.

Let a more than we are consume us, that a more than we are may survive us.

In every thou, a ray of the Eternal Thou shines through.

In life there is growth and diminishment. We must accept both, yet keep struggling against diminishment—nourished by the bread of earth, intoxicated by the wine of beauty, disciplined and made strong by the human struggle.

There is no not-holy, only the not-yet-hallowed.

There is no enemy, only the not yet befriended or reconciled.

True transmigration means reverence for persons, reverence for bugs, birds, flowers, fish, trees, and tigers of the jungle, reverence for the sacred cosmos whence we came and to which we return.

Notes

Foreword

1. Henry David Thoreau, *Walden* (Boston: Houghton, Mifflin & Company, 1893), p. 489.

Chapter 2

1. George Santayana, "The Poetry of Christian Dogma," in *Interpretations of Poetry and Religion* (New York: Harper Torchbooks, 1957), pp. 76–117. 2. *Ya-huva: O-He!* Martin Buber, *Moses* (Oxford: East & West Library, 1947), p. 50. 3. Rig-Veda 1:50. 4. Ibid. 1:124. 5. Ibid. 10:177. 6. Atharva-Veda 13:3. 7. Rig-Veda 10. 82:7. 8. Ibid. 10:129. 9. Ibid. 8:100.

Chapter 3

1. Bhagavad Gita 2:19–20. 2. Ibid. 2:22–23. 3. Katha Upanishad 1. 2:18–19. 4. Isa Upanishad 1. 4:4–5. 5. Chandogya Upanishad 6.9:4. 6. Ibid. 3. 14:2. 7. Katha Upanishad 6:12. 8. Brhad-

aranyaka Upanishad 5:1. 9. Ibid. 4. 4:7. 10. Ibid. 4.3:37. 11. Svetasvatara Upanishad 4:4. 12. Kena Upanishad 2:3. 13. Katha Upanishad 2. 2:12. 14. Bhagavad Gita 13:27.

Chapter 4

1. Vinaya Mahavagga 16:20. 2. Fo-Sho-Tsan-King 5. 25:1962–1964. 3. Tevigga Sutta 1:46. 4. Mahavagga 1:7–10. 5. Udana 8:3. 6. Maha Parinibbana Suttanta. 7. Udana 8:8. 8. Dhammapada 203.

Chapter 5

1. Mahavagga 1:5. 2. Coates and Ishizuka, *Honen, His Life and Teaching* (Kyoto, Japan: The Chion-In), pp. 580–81. 3. Cited by Karl Luvig Reichelt in *Truth and Tradition in Chinese Buddhism* (Shanhai, 1927).

Chapter 6

1. Malachi 1:2–3; cited by St. Paul in Romans 9:13 (KJV). 2. Brother Antoninus *Hazards of Holiness* (New York: Doubleday & Company, 1962). 3. Isaiah 2:1–4, slight variant from RSV.

Chapter 7

1. Mark 1:23–26 (KJV). 2. Gathas, Yasna 30:3. 3. Ibid. 45:2. 4. See "The Manual of Discipine" and "The War of the Sons of Light and the Sons of Darkness" in Theodore H. Gaster, *The Dead Sea*

Scriptures (New York: Doubleday Anchor Books, 1957). 5. Ephesians 6:12 (NEB). 6. Arnold Toynbee, *A Study of History* (London: Oxford University Press, 1934), X:143–44. 7. Subhadra Bhikshu, *A Buddhist Catechism* (New York: Brentano 1920). 8. Isaiah 45:7 (KJV).

Chapter 8

1. Boris Pasternak, *Doctor Zhivago* (New York: Pantheon Books, 1958), p. 43. 2. Galatians 3:26–29 (KJV). 3. Albert Schweitzer, *The Mysticism of Paul the Apostle* (New York: Henry Holt & Company, 1931). 4. Colossians 3:14 (KJV and NEB). 5. Galatians 6:15, Tillich's variant of RSV. 6. See "The New Being," sermon by Paul Tillich in the book of that title (New York: Charles Scribner's Sons, 1955), pp. 15–24. 7. Ibid., p. 19.

Chapter 9

1. Kornelis H. Miskotte, *When the Gods Are Silent* (New York: Harper & Row, 1967), p. 8. 2. Popovi Da, "Indian Pottery and Indian Values," in *Exploration 1970*, (Santa Fe, N.M.: School of American Research), pp. 3–7. 3. Ibid. 4. Tao Te Ching.

Chapter 10

1. See R. R. Marett, *The Sacraments of Simple Folk* (New York: Oxford University Press, 1933). 2. Martin Buber, *Hasidism* (New York: Philosophical Library, 1948), pp. 99–100. 3. Robinson Jeffers, "Look How Beautiful," in *The Beginning and the End*, (New York: Random House, 1954), p. 52. 4. Cited by Victor Gollancz in *Man and God*, (Boston: Houghton, Mifflin & Company, 1951)

from *Later Poems*, translated by J. B. Leishman (Hertfordshire, England: Hogarth Press, 1938). 5. Isaiah 40:6–8 (MODERN READERS BIBLE).

Chapter 11

1. Isaiah 60:10, 14 (KJV). 2. *The Best Stories of Wilbur Daniel Steele* (New York: Doubleday & Company, 1946), p. 198.

Chapter 12

1. See F. H. Balfour, trans. and ed., *The Works of Chuang-tse* (Shanghai: Kelly & Walsh, n.d.), pp. 178–81, or the selections from Chuang Tzu in Lin Yutang's *The Wisdom of India and China* (New York: Random House, 1942). 2. The Analects of Confucius, ch. 3. 3. Tao Te Ching, 47. 4. *The Wisdom of India and China*, p. 579. 5. Tao Te Ching, 22. 6. Ibid. 8. 7. Ibid. 78. 8. Ibid. 30. 9. Ibid. 46. 10. Ibid. 21. 11. Ibid. 69. 12. Ibid. 61. 13. Ibid. 17. 14. Ibid. 80. 15. Ibid. 35.

Chapter 13

1. Genesis 1:20 (KJV). 2. Ralph Waldo Emerson, "Experience," in *Essays*, second series. 3. Genesis 2:21–22 (KJV). 4. Jeremiah 5:31 (KJV). 5. Genesis 1:28 (KJV). 6. Psalm 49:11 (KJV). 7. Revelation 9:11 (KJV). 8. Ibid. 18:10. 9. Pierre Teilhard de Chardin, *The Future of Man* (New York: Harper & Row, 1964). 10. Genesis 1:31 (KJV).

Chapter 14

1. Walt Whitman, "Song of Myself."2. Wisdom, Apocrypha, 18:14–15.3. Martin Buber, "Hope for This Hour," address at Carnegie Hall, New York, 1952. See also "Genuine Dialogue" and "The Possibilities of Peace," in Maurice Friedman, trans. and ed. *Pointing the Way* (New York: Harper & Brothers, 1957).

Note on the selections from the great scriptures: Those from the Upanishads follow, with slight variations, the translation by Radhakrishnan in *The Principal Upanishads* (New York: Harper & Brothers, 1953). Selections from the Bhagavad Gita follow, with slight variations and a different arrangement, the version in *A Source Book of Indian Philosophy*, edited by S. Radhakrishnan and Charles A. Moore (Princeton: Princeton University Press, 1957). The selections from the Tao Te Ching are in my own version and arrangement, made after a careful study of a score of translations, with Arthur Waley, *The Way and Its Power* (London: George Allen & Unwin 1934) the basic guide. Buddhist and other citations from the great scriptures were taken from *Sacred Books of the East*, edited by F. Max Müller (Oxford: Clarendon Press, 1884).

73 74 75 10 9 8 7 6 5 4 3 2 1